Introduction

- The importance of model optimization for environments.

- Common challenges faced in deploying machine learning models.

- Overview of the book: Techniques, tools, and case studies to streamline and enhance model performance during deployment.

Chapter 1: Understanding Model Optimization

- What is model optimization?

- Key objectives: Reducing latency, minimizing resource usage, and maintaining accuracy.

- Trade-offs in optimization: Speed vs. accuracy, size vs. functionality.

Chapter 2: The Model Deployment Lifecycle

- From development to production: Steps in the lifecycle.

- Where optimization fits in the deployment process.

- Common bottlenecks during deployment.

Chapter 3: Optimization Techniques

3.1 Quantization

- Definition and types (e.g., dynamic, static, and post-training quantization).

- Advantages and limitations.

- Hands-on example: Quantizing a PyTorch model for deployment.

3.2 Pruning

- What is pruning, and why is it useful?
- Structured vs. unstructured pruning.
- Practical example: Pruning a TensorFlow model.

3.3 Knowledge Distillation

- Training smaller models to mimic larger ones.
- How it works and when to use it.
- Case study: Applying knowledge distillation to an NLP model.

3.4 Caching and Lazy Loading

- Optimizing data access patterns for serving.
- Implementing caching in RESTful APIs.

Chapter 4: Tools and Frameworks

4.1 TensorRT

- Overview and use cases.
- Example: Optimizing a deep learning model for GPU inference.

4.2 ONNX Runtime

- Why ONNX for cross-framework optimization?
- Hands-on: Converting a PyTorch model to ONNX and optimizing it.

4.3 TensorFlow Lite

- Optimizing for mobile and edge devices.

- Example: Deploying a TFLite model on an Android app.

4.4 Apache TVM

- Compilation for multiple hardware backends.

- Step-by-step: Using TVM to optimize a model for ARM processors.

Chapter 5: Hardware-Specific Optimization

- CPU vs. GPU vs. TPU: How hardware impacts optimization.

- Strategies for hardware-aware optimization.

- Example: Profiling and optimizing a model for NVIDIA GPUs.

Chapter 6: Scaling and Monitoring

6.1 Scaling Models in Production

- Horizontal vs. vertical scaling.

- Load balancing and autoscaling strategies.

6.2 Monitoring Performance

- Metrics to track: Latency, throughput, error rates.

- Tools for monitoring: Prometheus, Grafana, and APMs.

Chapter 7: Real-World Case Studies

Case Study 1: Optimizing a Vision Model for Real-Time Inference

- Problem: High latency in an object detection application.

- Solution: Using TensorRT and quantization to achieve a 5x speedup.

Case Study 2: Reducing Costs for a Chatbot Model

  - Problem: High cloud costs due to inefficient resource usage.

  - Solution: Pruning and distillation to reduce model size by 50%.

Case Study 3: Scaling an E-Commerce Recommendation System

  - Problem: Latency spikes during peak hours.

  - Solution: Implementing caching and hardware-aware optimizations.

Chapter 8: Future Trends in Model Optimization

  - The rise of AI hardware accelerators.

  - AutoML and automated optimization pipelines.

  - The role of edge computing in optimization.

Conclusion

  - Recap of key optimization techniques and tools.

  - The importance of continuous monitoring and improvement.

  - Encouragement to experiment and adapt strategies based on use cases.

Appendices

  - **Appendix A**: Glossary of Optimization Terms.

  - **Appendix B**: List of Tools and Libraries.

- **Appendix C**: Additional Resources and Reading.

Introduction

In a world increasingly driven by data and powered by artificial intelligence, deploying machine learning models that are both reliable and efficient has become critical to business success. Yet, moving a model from the research phase into a real-world production environment is no small feat. Resource constraints, latency demands, and unpredictable traffic spikes can all create bottlenecks that derail even the most promising AI initiatives. This book is designed to guide you through the maze of challenges associated with deployment and introduce you to battle-tested techniques that optimize your models for speed, memory efficiency, and cost-effectiveness—without sacrificing accuracy.

We begin by highlighting why model optimization is essential for production environments, where milliseconds of latency can mean the difference between winning and losing a customer. Next, we explore the full deployment lifecycle, pinpointing the critical junctures where optimization yields the greatest return on investment. Building on this foundation, we dive deep into various optimization strategies—from quantization and pruning to knowledge distillation and caching—and illustrate how each can be leveraged to meet specific performance and resource requirements.

Along the way, you'll learn about powerful tools and frameworks such as TensorRT, ONNX Runtime, TensorFlow Lite, and Apache TVM, which simplify the optimization process and help you adapt your models for different hardware backends. We also cover the intricacies of hardware-specific optimizations, scaling techniques, and monitoring best practices, giving you a holistic view of what it takes to keep your models operating at peak efficiency. Real-world case studies demonstrate how these optimizations translate to tangible gains in speed, cost savings, and user satisfaction, while a glimpse into future trends—like specialized AI hardware and automated optimization pipelines—rounds out our exploration.

Whether you are a data scientist, software engineer, or technical leader, this book will serve as your roadmap to navigating the complexities of machine learning deployments. By combining theoretical underpinnings with hands-on examples and best practices, **Optimizing Machine Learning Models for Deployment** empowers you to harness the full potential of AI in a production setting—today and in the dynamic environment of tomorrow.

Chapter 1: Understanding Model Optimization

Model optimization is the cornerstone of successful machine learning deployments. In today's fast-paced, data-driven environments, it's not enough to build a highly accurate model; you also need to ensure that it can run efficiently under real-world constraints. This chapter lays the groundwork for why and how we optimize machine learning models, detailing the core objectives and the delicate balance between them. By the end of this chapter, you should have a firm grasp on what optimization entails, why it is critical, and the fundamental trade-offs that come into play.

1.1 Introduction

Machine learning models can vary significantly in complexity, from simple linear regressions to deep neural networks containing millions—or even billions—of parameters. When you train a model in a research or lab setting, the primary concern is often achieving the highest possible accuracy or best possible performance metric (e.g., F1-score, mean average precision). However, when that same model needs to run in a production environment—serving thousands or even millions of requests per second—considerations such as speed, memory usage, scalability, and cost become equally, if not more, important.

Model optimization bridges the gap between a proof-of-concept model in a notebook and a production-grade model that delivers consistent results under strict time and resource constraints. Without effective optimization strategies, your application can suffer from lagging response times, unpredictable resource usage, and even system failures. Moreover, poorly optimized models can incur unnecessary costs, especially when you're running on cloud infrastructure that charges for compute time and memory usage.

1.2 What Is Model Optimization?

In its simplest form, **model optimization** refers to a series of techniques and strategies aimed at improving a model's operational characteristics—such as inference speed, memory footprint, and power consumption—while preserving (or minimally impacting) its predictive accuracy. These techniques can be as straightforward as reducing the precision of floating-point calculations or as sophisticated as transforming the computational graph of a neural network to execute more efficiently on specialized hardware.

Broadly, model optimization can be viewed from two angles:

1. **Algorithmic Optimization**: Changes to the model architecture or how the model is trained. For example, knowledge distillation trains a smaller student model to mimic a larger teacher model's behavior. Pruning removes redundant connections within a network, streamlining its structure without significant loss of accuracy.

2. **Implementation-Level Optimization**: Changes to the way the model's computations are executed at runtime. This includes leveraging faster libraries (like NVIDIA's TensorRT), adopting lower-precision arithmetic (such as quantization), or using optimized graph compilers (like Apache TVM) that map operations more efficiently onto specific hardware.

In real-world deployments, both algorithmic and implementation-level optimizations are often combined to achieve maximum gains.

1.3 Key Objectives of Model Optimization

While there are various reasons to optimize a model, three overarching objectives tend to dominate production scenarios:

1.3.1 Reducing Latency

Latency is the time it takes for a model to produce an output after receiving an input. For many applications—particularly real-time services like fraud detection, autonomous vehicles, or real-time translations—latency is a critical factor. A delay of even a few milliseconds can be unacceptable if it cascades through a mission-critical system. Optimizing for latency often involves techniques like:

- **Quantization**: Using lower-precision data types (e.g., 8-bit integers instead of 32-bit floats) to speed up arithmetic operations.
- **GPU/TPU Acceleration**: Exploiting parallel processing capabilities of specialized hardware.
- **Caching and Batching**: Caching intermediate computations or batching multiple inputs together to utilize hardware resources more efficiently.

1.3.2 Minimizing Resource Usage

Resource usage covers everything from CPU and GPU cycles to memory footprint and power consumption. In a cloud environment, these translate directly to operating costs; every additional gigabyte of RAM or GPU hour adds to the bottom line. On mobile or edge devices, limited computational resources and battery life make resource efficiency critical. Common approaches to reducing resource usage include:

- **Pruning and Structural Optimization**: Removing parameters or entire layers in a controlled way.
- **Knowledge Distillation**: Training a smaller model that approximates the performance of a larger model.

- **Serverless Architecture**: Employing serverless inference solutions that dynamically scale resources up or down depending on load.

1.3.3 Maintaining Accuracy

All optimization efforts must be balanced against the need to maintain a certain level of **accuracy** or other performance metrics. If you prune a model too aggressively or quantize parameters too coarsely, you may introduce large accuracy drops that negate any benefits of improved speed or reduced memory. The key is **measured** optimization—understanding your application's tolerance for reduced accuracy and ensuring that any losses are within acceptable bounds.

1.4 Trade-Offs in Optimization

Optimizing machine learning models is rarely a zero-sum game; every gain in speed or reduced memory can potentially come at the cost of accuracy, model interpretability, or additional engineering overhead. Let's explore some of the most common trade-offs.

1.4.1 Speed vs. Accuracy

One of the most classic trade-offs is between **speed (latency)** and **accuracy**. When you reduce floating-point precision or prune large chunks of a network, you often make your model faster. However, these same techniques can also introduce numerical errors or remove valuable information, negatively affecting accuracy. The decision of how much accuracy you can afford to lose depends on your application domain:

- **High-Stakes Scenarios**: In medical diagnosis or autonomous driving, a slight drop in accuracy can lead to catastrophic outcomes. Here, you may sacrifice speed for guaranteed accuracy.
- **Consumer Applications**: For recommender systems or social media applications, a small decrease in

accuracy may be acceptable if it results in significantly faster response times and better user experience.

1.4.2 Size vs. Functionality

Pruning and knowledge distillation can drastically reduce the size of a model, making it easier to deploy on resource-constrained devices. However, smaller models might be less expressive and sometimes cannot capture all the nuances of a larger model. This trade-off becomes especially important in scenarios where:

- **Edge Devices**: Deploying a model on a smartphone or IoT device with limited RAM.
- **Variable Feature Sets**: Reducing model complexity might force you to remove certain features or layers that capture critical patterns in the data.

1.4.3 The Balancing Act

In practice, teams often approach model optimization as a **balancing act**—iteratively applying optimization techniques, measuring impact on performance metrics and resource usage, and then deciding whether further optimization is still worthwhile. If you have a model that is 95% accurate, a 2% drop for a 10x speedup might be acceptable in many applications. But if that 2% drop costs millions in lost revenue or significantly impacts user trust, it's no longer a good deal.

It's critical to keep in mind that optimization should be guided by concrete metrics and business or application requirements. Without a clear definition of what "acceptable performance" means in your context, you risk either under-optimizing or over-optimizing your models.

1.5 Why Does Model Optimization Matter?

To fully appreciate the importance of model optimization, it helps to consider a range of practical scenarios:

- **Real-Time Recommendations**: Online retailers often need to serve product recommendations within fractions of a second. An unoptimized model can lead to noticeable delays, resulting in a poor user experience and lost sales.
- **Cost-Effective Cloud Operations**: Organizations that handle millions of requests daily often rely on cloud-based solutions like AWS or Google Cloud. Efficiently optimized models can significantly lower compute costs, saving large sums of money every month.
- **Edge and Mobile Applications**: From smartphones to self-driving cars, edge devices are becoming increasingly prevalent. These devices have limited memory and compute capabilities, making model optimization a necessity to run advanced AI features.
- **Large-Scale AI Services**: Companies offering software-as-a-service (SaaS) platforms need to optimize their models to serve multiple clients simultaneously, each with different workloads and SLAs (Service Level Agreements).

In all these cases, model optimization translates to tangible benefits: faster inference speeds, lower costs, and broader deployment possibilities.

1.6 How Optimization Fits Into the Deployment Lifecycle

You might wonder, at which stage in the machine learning lifecycle should you consider model optimization? While the entire **Chapter 2** explores the lifecycle in more detail, here is a brief overview:

1. **Research and Development**: During experimentation, you aim for the highest accuracy or best performance metrics.
2. **Pre-Deployment**: Once a model meets basic accuracy thresholds, you start exploring optimization techniques (like pruning or quantization) to see how they impact performance.
3. **Production Deployment**: You integrate the optimized model into your service or product. This step involves thorough testing, continuous integration, and monitoring.
4. **Monitoring and Iteration**: After deployment, you track key performance indicators (KPIs) such as latency, error rates, and CPU/GPU usage. Further optimization may be required as usage scales or new features are introduced.

Thinking of optimization as a continuous process rather than a one-time task helps you remain agile in the face of changing requirements and technologies.

1.7 Conclusion and What's Next

Model optimization is about more than just shaving milliseconds off your inference time or squeezing your model into a smaller memory footprint. It's a strategic imperative that touches every phase of the machine learning deployment lifecycle, from initial research to production and beyond. By understanding the core objectives—reducing latency, minimizing resource usage, and maintaining accuracy—and the trade-offs involved, you're better equipped to make decisions that align with your project's goals.

In the next chapter, **Chapter 2: The Model Deployment Lifecycle**, we'll take a step-by-step look at how a model moves from a data scientist's notebook into a production environment, highlighting the points at which optimization can have the most significant impact. You'll gain an overview of the common bottlenecks and learn to identify where optimization should be a priority. As you progress through the book, you'll discover practical techniques—from quantization and pruning to specialized tooling and hardware accelerators—and see how they can be applied to real-world scenarios.

By the time you complete this journey, you'll be fully equipped to bring your models into production environments that demand both peak performance and reliability, ensuring that your machine learning initiatives deliver lasting value to your organization and your users.

Key Takeaways

1. **Model optimization** is essential to adapt machine learning models for real-world constraints, such as latency requirements and limited computational resources.
2. The **three core objectives**—reducing latency, minimizing resource usage, and maintaining accuracy—guide most optimization efforts.
3. **Trade-offs** are inevitable; you often exchange some level of model accuracy for improvements in speed, size, or cost.
4. Optimization is **context-dependent**. The acceptable balance of speed, accuracy, and size varies by application and domain.
5. **Continuous iteration** is crucial. As your application scales and requirements evolve, re-evaluating and re-optimizing your models is necessary to maintain efficiency.

With this foundation in place, we can move forward into the lifecycle of model deployment, which sets the stage for understanding **where** and **when** to apply the optimization techniques covered in later chapters.

Chapter 2: The model deployment lifecycle

Deploying a machine learning model from a data scientist's local environment into a fully operational production system involves many moving parts. While training the model itself is often the most visible phase, a great deal of work must happen before, during, and after this step to ensure that the model meets real-world performance, reliability, and scalability requirements. This chapter provides a step-by-step look at the **model deployment lifecycle**, discussing the common stages, typical bottlenecks, and—most importantly—where and how **optimization** plays a crucial role throughout the process.

2.1 Introduction

In the world of machine learning, the term "deployment" can mean different things depending on context. For some, it refers to the moment a trained model is placed on a server to handle live traffic. For others, deployment encompasses the broader process of integrating a model into a full software system, complete with data pipelines, monitoring, and maintenance procedures.

Regardless of the exact definition, the deployment lifecycle can be broken down into **distinct phases** that guide you from initial data exploration all the way to monitoring a live service. Each phase presents its own challenges and opportunities for optimization. In this chapter, we outline these phases, highlight where optimization typically fits, and delve into the common bottlenecks that can arise when transitioning from an offline setting to a production environment.

2.2 Phases of the Model Deployment Lifecycle

While different organizations may have variations in naming and structure, most model deployment processes include the following phases:

1. **Data Collection and Preprocessing**
2. **Model Development (Training and Validation)**
3. **Pre-Deployment Planning and Optimization**
4. **Production Deployment**
5. **Monitoring and Maintenance**

Let's explore each phase in more detail.

2.2.1 Data Collection and Preprocessing

Overview

- **Data Collection**: Gathering relevant data, whether from operational databases, real-time logs, or external APIs.
- **Data Cleaning**: Removing duplicates, handling missing values, and correcting errors.
- **Feature Engineering**: Transforming raw data into features that improve model performance (e.g., normalizing values, creating aggregated metrics).

Although this stage seems primarily focused on data, the choices you make here can **significantly** affect downstream optimization opportunities. For instance, capturing high-dimensional features with low variance can lead to unnecessarily large models. Conversely, simplifying features —or using dimensionality reduction techniques—can yield more compact, faster models down the line.

Role of Optimization

- **Optimized Feature Selection**: By selecting a smaller, more relevant set of features, you can reduce the size of your model and speed up training and inference times.

- **Efficient Data Pipelines**: Building efficient, automated data pipelines ensures that when the model eventually goes live, the data feeding it is processed quickly and reliably—reducing the risk of deployment bottlenecks.

2.2.2 Model Development (Training and Validation)

Overview

- **Model Selection**: Choosing the right algorithm or architecture (e.g., neural networks, gradient-boosted trees, or classical regression models) based on the problem and available data.
- **Training**: Iteratively updating the model parameters to minimize a loss function on the training data.
- **Validation**: Measuring the model's performance on unseen data to guard against overfitting and ensure generalizability.

This is typically where data scientists focus the majority of their efforts. The main objective is to achieve strong predictive performance. However, once you begin considering real-world constraints (such as latency requirements and hardware limitations), you might incorporate **lightweight forms of optimization** early on.

Role of Optimization

- **Early Exploration of Lightweight Architectures**: Instead of starting with the largest possible model, some teams begin by exploring simpler or smaller architectures to see if they meet baseline performance requirements.
- **Hyperparameter Tuning for Efficiency**: Tuning hyperparameters not just for accuracy but also for

computational efficiency. For example, smaller batch sizes might reduce memory usage at the expense of longer training times, which might be acceptable if it leads to a more deployable model.

2.2.3 Pre-Deployment Planning and Optimization

Overview

Before finalizing the model for deployment, you typically engage in a period of **pre-deployment planning**. This is where you consider your runtime environment—be it a cloud-based server, on-premise cluster, mobile device, or edge hardware—and figure out how to best adapt the model to that environment.

- **Environment Considerations**: Identifying the target hardware (CPU, GPU, TPU, or specialized accelerators) and software frameworks (TensorFlow, PyTorch, ONNX, etc.).
- **Performance Budgets**: Setting strict targets for latency, throughput, and memory usage.
- **Resource Constraints**: Understanding the memory, power, and processing limitations of your deployment environment.

This is also the phase where you can apply many of the **optimization techniques** discussed in later chapters (quantization, pruning, distillation, graph optimizations) to ensure that your model meets your production criteria without sacrificing too much accuracy.

Role of Optimization

- **Quantization and Pruning**: Reducing model size and improving inference speed.
- **Knowledge Distillation**: Training a smaller "student" model to mimic a larger "teacher" model.

- **Caching and Data Pipeline Optimizations**: Ensuring your model's inputs can be processed quickly and efficiently during live inference.

2.2.4 Production Deployment

Overview

With the model tuned and optimized, the next step is **production deployment**—integrating the model into a live environment. This phase can vary dramatically depending on whether the deployment is:

- **Batch**: The model processes large volumes of data periodically (e.g., end-of-day risk assessment, weekly analytics).
- **Real-Time or Online**: The model must respond to incoming requests in milliseconds or seconds (e.g., fraud detection, recommendation systems).
- **Edge or Mobile**: The model runs locally on a device with limited compute resources (e.g., a smartphone or an embedded system in a factory).

Each scenario has unique constraints that can affect how you continue to optimize the model. For instance, a cloud-based service might focus on scaling horizontally to handle high request volumes, whereas an edge deployment might emphasize power efficiency and extremely small model sizes.

Role of Optimization

- **Containerization and Microservices**: Packaging the model in a lightweight container (e.g., Docker) and deploying it via microservices to easily scale and update.
- **Load Testing**: Stress-testing the model to ensure it meets latency and throughput targets under peak load.
- **Hardware-Specific Tuning**: Using specialized frameworks like TensorRT, ONNX Runtime, or

hardware accelerators (e.g., GPUs, TPUs, FPGAs) to squeeze out maximum performance.

2.2.5 Monitoring and Maintenance

Overview

Once the model is live, the work isn't over. **Monitoring** and **maintenance** are critical for long-term success. Models can drift over time as real-world data evolves, requiring retraining or recalibration. Infrastructure can change, demand patterns can shift, and new features may need to be introduced.

- **Monitoring**: Tracking metrics like latency, throughput, error rates, and accuracy in production.
- **Logging and Alerting**: Setting up alerts for anomalies in performance or data distribution that might indicate issues like data drift or model degradation.
- **Feedback Loops and Retraining**: Using production data to periodically retrain or fine-tune the model, ensuring it remains relevant and accurate.

Role of Optimization

- **Continuous Optimization**: As data evolves or usage scales, you may need to revisit quantization levels, pruning strategies, or even switch to more advanced techniques like dynamic batch sizing.
- **A/B Testing**: Experimenting with different model optimizations in production to see which ones yield the best performance-accuracy trade-off for real users.
- **Canary Deployments**: Releasing an updated, optimized model to a small subset of users first, ensuring stability before a full rollout.

2.3 Where Optimization Fits in the Deployment Process

Although we mentioned optimization touchpoints in each phase, it's worth zooming in on **where optimization has the most significant impact**:

1. **During Model Development**: Incorporating efficiency metrics early can help avoid building overly large or slow models that are difficult to optimize later.
2. **Immediately Before Deployment**: This is often the largest optimization push, where teams apply pruning, quantization, or other methods to meet strict production goals.
3. **Post-Deployment / Monitoring**: As the model is used in production, new opportunities for optimization— like caching or changing batch sizes—may arise based on real usage patterns.

Many organizations treat optimization as a **continuous, iterative process** rather than a one-off task. This means regularly reassessing whether the deployed model still meets its performance and cost targets and adjusting accordingly.

2.4 Common Bottlenecks During Deployment

The journey to production isn't without pitfalls. Here are some of the most common bottlenecks you might face—and how optimization strategies can help overcome them:

2.4.1 High Latency

Symptoms: Users experience slow responses, or batch jobs take too long to complete.

Causes:

- Excessive model complexity (too many layers or parameters).

- Inefficient computation graph or data type usage.
- Non-optimal hardware utilization.

Possible Solutions:

- **Quantization** to reduce data precision.
- **Pruning** to remove unnecessary parameters.
- **Caching** frequently accessed data or intermediate computations.
- **GPU/TPU Offloading** if the current hardware is CPU-bound.

2.4.2 Resource Exhaustion and Scaling Limits

Symptoms: The system runs out of CPU/GPU memory, or costs skyrocket due to excessive resource usage under load.

Causes:

- Large models that require significant memory or compute power.
- Inability to scale horizontally or vertically due to infrastructure constraints.
- Inefficient data pipelines that create bottlenecks.

Possible Solutions:

- **Knowledge Distillation** to shrink model size.
- **Autoscaling** strategies in the cloud.
- **Distributed serving** to handle peaks in traffic.
- **Efficient batching** of requests for higher throughput.

2.4.3 Model Degradation Over Time (Concept Drift)

Symptoms: Prediction accuracy declines as real-world data shifts away from the training distribution.

Causes:

- Data distribution changes due to seasonality, market shifts, or new user behavior.
- Model hasn't been retrained or updated to reflect current conditions.

Possible Solutions:

- **Periodic retraining** or fine-tuning with updated data.
- **Active learning** to continuously gather new training examples.
- **Adaptive optimization** that adjusts parameters on-the-fly (though more advanced and less commonly used).

2.4.4 Integration and Compatibility Issues

Symptoms: Deployment fails due to mismatched library versions, incompatibility between frameworks, or difficulty moving the model across different environments.

Causes:

- Using multiple different machine learning frameworks (e.g., TensorFlow for training and PyTorch for inference) without a standard intermediary format.
- Insufficient containerization or environment testing.

Possible Solutions:

- **ONNX** (Open Neural Network Exchange) for cross-framework model compatibility.
- **Docker or Kubernetes** to ensure consistent environments.
- Thorough **CI/CD pipelines** that automate integration testing.

2.5 The Bigger Picture: MLOps and Continuous Deployment

In recent years, the concept of **MLOps** (Machine Learning Operations) has gained traction, highlighting the need to apply DevOps best practices—like continuous integration, continuous deployment (CI/CD), and infrastructure as code—to machine learning projects. MLOps frameworks help automate much of the deployment lifecycle, from data acquisition to monitoring.

2.5.1 Benefits of MLOps

- **Automated Testing**: Integration tests that ensure new model versions are compatible with existing systems.
- **Version Control**: Tracking changes to data, model code, and hyperparameters.
- **Reproducibility**: The ability to reconstruct the model training environment for debugging or auditing purposes.
- **Scalability**: Automated scaling policies that allocate resources dynamically as demand changes.

2.5.2 Incorporating Optimization in MLOps Pipelines

MLOps pipelines can include **optimization scripts** that run after model training but before deployment. This automated approach ensures that every new model version passes through the same set of optimization and validation checks, reducing the risk of performance regressions.

2.6 Conclusion and What's Next

Deploying a machine learning model is a multi-stage process that extends well beyond simply training a model. Each phase —from data collection and feature engineering to live monitoring—presents unique challenges and opportunities for optimization. By recognizing these phases and anticipating common bottlenecks, you can develop a deployment strategy that ensures your model meets real-world performance, scalability, and reliability requirements.

As you move forward in this book, you'll gain deeper insights into **specific optimization techniques**, from **quantization** and **pruning** to **knowledge distillation** and **caching mechanisms**. In the next chapter, we'll explore these techniques in detail, showing you how to systematically reduce model size and inference time. Along the way, we'll circle back to the deployment lifecycle framework, illustrating exactly how each optimization method can slot into your development and deployment workflow.

Key Takeaways

1. **Deployment is a Lifecycle**: From data collection to monitoring, each phase has unique challenges and optimization considerations.
2. **Optimization Happens Continuously**: While there is often a major optimization push right before production, tuning can and should happen at multiple lifecycle stages.
3. **Common Bottlenecks**: Latency, resource constraints, model drift, and integration issues often arise, and there are specific optimization strategies to address each.
4. **MLOps**: Integrating best practices like CI/CD and version control streamlines the deployment process and helps automate repetitive tasks, including optimization checks.
5. **Next Steps**: With an understanding of where optimization fits in, you're ready to dive into the **techniques** themselves. Chapter 3 will cover quantization, pruning, knowledge distillation, and more, showing you how to systematically reduce your model's footprint without sacrificing critical accuracy.

By mastering the deployment lifecycle and the role of optimization within it, you'll be better equipped to deliver machine learning models that excel both in **offline** and **online** environments.

Chapter 3: Optimization Techniques

In the previous chapters, we discussed the critical role that optimization plays in the model deployment lifecycle and explored where optimization efforts can yield the greatest return on investment. Now, we dive into the **practical techniques** you can use to optimize your machine learning models. While these methods differ in their specific approaches, they share a common goal: **to improve inference speed, reduce resource consumption, and maintain acceptable accuracy** levels.

This chapter covers four major techniques:

1. **Quantization** – Reducing the precision of model parameters to decrease computation and memory usage.
2. **Pruning** – Removing redundant or unimportant parameters from a model to make it lighter and faster.
3. **Knowledge Distillation** – Transferring the "knowledge" of a large model into a smaller, more efficient one.
4. **Caching and Lazy Loading** – Optimizing data and inference paths to reduce overhead and latency.

By the end of this chapter, you will have a detailed understanding of each technique, including when to use them, the trade-offs, and **hands-on examples** illustrating their practical applications.

3.1 Quantization

3.1.1 What Is Quantization?

Quantization involves transforming a model's parameters (and sometimes activations) from higher-precision floating-point representations (e.g., 32-bit floating point, also known as FP32) to lower-precision formats (e.g., 16-bit, 8-bit, or even integer formats). The primary objective is to **reduce the computational complexity and memory footprint**.

When you quantize weights and activations, you generally store (and in some cases, compute) them in lower-bit representations. This can lead to faster inference because **integer arithmetic** (INT8 or INT16) typically runs more quickly on modern hardware than floating-point arithmetic.

3.1.2 Types of Quantization

1. **Post-Training Quantization (PTQ)**

   - **Definition**: Converting a trained FP32 model to a lower-precision model after the training process is complete.
   - **Pros**: Straightforward to implement; no retraining required.
   - **Cons**: May introduce noticeable accuracy degradation, especially if the model is highly sensitive to small numeric changes.

2. **Quantization-Aware Training (QAT)**

   - **Definition**: Simulating lower-precision arithmetic during training so that the model adapts to the quantized representation.
   - **Pros**: Usually yields better accuracy compared to PTQ because the model "learns" how to handle quantized weights and activations.
   - **Cons**: Requires additional training time and effort, along with changes to the training pipeline.

3. **Dynamic Quantization**

   - **Definition**: Quantizing only certain parts of the model (often activations) at inference time, based on the data range observed dynamically.
   - **Pros**: Often used for RNNs and Transformers where activation ranges vary; easy to

implement in many frameworks (e.g., PyTorch `dynamic_quantization`).

- **Cons**: Might not provide as significant a speedup as full quantization (weights + activations).

4. **Static Quantization**

- **Definition**: Using calibration data to determine the range of activations and then applying fixed quantization parameters.
- **Pros**: Can achieve consistently low memory usage and predictable performance gains.
- **Cons**: Requires an extra calibration step that needs representative data.

3.1.3 Advantages and Limitations

- **Advantages**:

  - **Reduced Model Size**: Storing weights in INT8 instead of FP32 can cut memory usage by up to 75%.
  - **Faster Inference**: Integer operations are typically more efficient on CPUs and many GPUs.
  - **Power Efficiency**: Especially beneficial on edge devices with limited power budgets.

- **Limitations**:

  - **Accuracy Drop**: Improper quantization can cause a noticeable decrease in accuracy.
  - **Hardware/Framework Support**: Full benefits require hardware that accelerates low-precision arithmetic and frameworks that provide robust quantization tooling.
  - **Complexity**: Some advanced quantization techniques (like QAT) require specialized knowledge and additional training steps.

3.1.4 Hands-On Example: Quantizing a PyTorch Model

1. **Train or Load a Model**

```python
import torch
import torchvision.models as models

# Load a pre-trained ResNet18 model
model = models.resnet18(pretrained=True)
model.eval()  # Set to evaluation mode
```

2. **Apply Dynamic Quantization** (as a simple demonstration)

```python
# Dynamic quantization for the linear layers
model_quantized =
torch.quantization.quantize_dynamic(
    model,  # The model to quantize
    {torch.nn.Linear},  # Layers to quantize
    dtype=torch.qint8  # Quantization data
type
)
```

3. Measure Performance

```python
# Compare inference times
import time

dummy_input = torch.randn(1, 3, 224, 224)

start_time = time.time()
with torch.no_grad():
    for _ in range(100):
        _ = model(dummy_input)
fp32_time = time.time() - start_time

start_time = time.time()
with torch.no_grad():
    for _ in range(100):
        _ = model_quantized(dummy_input)
int8_time = time.time() - start_time

print("FP32 Inference Time:
{:.4f}s".format(fp32_time))
print("INT8 Inference Time:
{:.4f}s".format(int8_time))
```

4. **Validate Accuracy**

- Run a test dataset inference and compare FP32 vs. INT8 performance metrics.
- If the accuracy drop is unacceptable, consider quantization-aware training or calibration methods.

This simple example demonstrates how easy it can be to get started with quantization in a modern framework like PyTorch. For more complex scenarios, you might explore **Quantization-Aware Training** or carefully tune the quantization parameters to minimize accuracy loss.

3.2 Pruning

3.2.1 What Is Pruning?

Pruning is the process of **removing parameters (weights or neurons) that contribute little** to a model's output. Neural networks, especially deep ones, can be highly over-parameterized, meaning that many weights have minimal impact on final predictions. By pruning these superfluous connections, you can **reduce the model's size** and often speed up inference.

3.2.2 Types of Pruning

1. **Unstructured Pruning**

   - **Definition**: Removes individual weights based on a criterion (e.g., smallest absolute weights).
   - **Pros**: Potentially removes a large fraction of parameters, leading to a very sparse weight matrix.
   - **Cons**: Sparse matrices can be hard to accelerate unless you have specialized hardware or libraries that exploit sparsity.

2. **Structured Pruning**

   - **Definition**: Removes entire filters, channels, or blocks to maintain a more compact structure.

- **Pros**: Easier to accelerate on standard hardware because the resulting model has fewer filters or channels, simplifying the architecture.
- **Cons**: May require more careful experimentation to find the right filters or channels to prune without harming accuracy.

3. **Layer-Wise Pruning**

- **Definition**: Pruning specific layers (often the largest or most redundant) while leaving others untouched.
- **Pros**: Targeted approach that focuses on the layers that contribute most to model size and latency.
- **Cons**: Requires a deep understanding of which layers are truly the bottleneck in your model.

3.2.3 Why Is Pruning Useful?

- **Model Size Reduction**: Fewer parameters mean less memory required for storage.
- **Potential Speedup**: If the pruned architecture is implemented efficiently, it can lead to faster inference.
- **Regularization**: Mild pruning can act like a regularizer, sometimes improving generalization by removing overfitted weights.

3.2.4 Practical Example: Pruning a TensorFlow Model

1. **Train or Load a Model**

```
import tensorflow as tf
from tensorflow.keras.applications import
MobileNetV2

model = MobileNetV2(weights='imagenet')
model.summary()
```

2. **Apply Pruning Schedules**
TensorFlow Model Optimization Toolkit provides built-in pruning capabilities:

```
from
tensorflow_model_optimization.sparsity.keras
import prune_low_magnitude, PolynomialDecay

pruning_params = {
    'pruning_schedule': PolynomialDecay(
        initial_sparsity=0.0,
        final_sparsity=0.50,
        begin_step=0,
        end_step=1000
    )
}

# Prune the entire model
pruned_model = prune_low_magnitude(model,
**pruning_params)
```

3. Retrain the pruned model

```
pruned_model.compile(
    optimizer=tf.keras.optimizers.Adam(),
    loss='categorical_crossentropy',
    metrics=['accuracy']
)

# Example training with a small dataset
# (In practice, use your full training set)
pruned_model.fit(train_data, train_labels,
epochs=5, validation_data=(val_data,
val_labels))
```

4. Strip Pruning Wrappers and Evaluate

After pruning, you can strip the pruning wrappers to create a final, smaller model:

```
from
tensorflow_model_optimization.sparsity.keras
import strip_pruning

final_model = strip_pruning(pruned_model)
final_model.save('pruned_mobilenet.h5')
```

- Validate the model's performance on your test dataset.
- Compare the new size and latency to the original MobileNetV2.

3.3 Knowledge Distillation

3.3.1 What Is Knowledge Distillation?

Knowledge Distillation is a technique where you **train a smaller "student" model to mimic the behavior of a larger "teacher" model**. The teacher model is often a high-capacity network that achieves state-of-the-art performance but is too large or slow for production. By using the teacher's outputs (or intermediate representations) as "soft labels," the student learns the teacher's function in a way that often exceeds the performance you'd get if you simply trained the smaller model from scratch.

3.3.2 How Does It Work?

1. **Teacher Model**: A large, accurate model (e.g., a BERT-large for NLP tasks).
2. **Student Model**: A smaller, more efficient model (e.g., a compact Transformer or a smaller CNN).
3. **Distillation Process**:
   - Use the teacher to generate probabilities (or logits) for training examples.
   - Train the student to match the teacher's outputs using a distillation loss, such as **KL Divergence** between the student's and teacher's outputs.
   - Optionally combine the distillation loss with the standard cross-entropy loss on the true labels.

3.3.3 Why Distillation?

- **Smaller Student Model**: Allows for deployment on resource-constrained devices.
- **Preserves Accuracy**: Student models often retain most of the teacher's accuracy—sometimes matching or exceeding it if trained carefully.
- **Faster Inference**: Ideal for real-time applications where latency is critical.

3.3.4 Case Study: Applying Knowledge Distillation to an NLP Model

1. **Teacher Model**: A large BERT or GPT-based language model.

2. **Student Model**: A DistilBERT or MobileBERT with significantly fewer parameters.

3. **Distillation Data**: Original training data (text corpus) + teacher's "soft" labels (the probability distribution over the vocabulary).

4. **Training Setup**:

```
from transformers import
BertForSequenceClassification,
DistilBertForSequenceClassification

# Teacher
teacher_model =
BertForSequenceClassification.from_pretraine
d("bert-base-uncased")
teacher_model.eval()

# Student
student_model =
DistilBertForSequenceClassification.from_pre
trained("distilbert-base-uncased")

# Distillation Loss
# Typically a combination of KL Divergence
on teacher logits and cross-entropy on true
labels.
```

5. **Training Loop**:

   - For each batch:
       1. Pass inputs through the teacher model to get logits.
       2. Pass the same inputs through the student model to get student logits.
       3. Compute **KL Divergence** between student and teacher logits.
       4. Compute cross-entropy with true labels.
       5. Combine losses and backpropagate.

6. **Evaluation**:

- Compare accuracy, F1 score, or other relevant metrics on a validation or test set.
- Measure inference speed on target hardware (CPU, GPU, or mobile device).

Knowledge distillation can transform an infeasible model into one that is lightweight enough for real-world deployment, all while retaining a large portion of the teacher's performance.

3.4 Caching and Lazy Loading

3.4.1 Why Cache?

While the previous sections focused on optimizing **model** parameters, there are also significant gains to be had from optimizing **data access** and **serving patterns**. **Caching** is one of the simplest yet most effective ways to reduce redundant computations and improve latency, especially in web or API-based deployments.

- **Definition**: Storing the results of frequently requested computations so that subsequent requests can be served more quickly.
- **Example**: Caching the output of a pre-processing step or even the final inference result for a given input if it's requested repeatedly.

3.4.2 Types of Caching

1. **Result Caching**

    - **Scenario**: An e-commerce recommendation system that serves the same recommendations to many similar user segments.
    - **Approach**: Store the recommended items for each segment in a cache (e.g., Redis or Memcached), and serve them without re-running the model.

2. **Intermediate Caching**

- **Scenario**: A complex pipeline with multiple transformations (e.g., text normalization, feature extraction).
- **Approach**: Cache intermediate steps, so repeated transformations are not re-computed each time.

3. **Feature Store**

- **Scenario**: Large-scale production systems that frequently re-use the same engineered features across multiple models.
- **Approach**: Build or use a dedicated feature store (like Feast) that caches and manages features at scale.

3.4.3 Lazy Loading

Lazy Loading delays the loading or computation of a resource until it's absolutely necessary. In the context of machine learning deployments:

- **Model Components**: If your model architecture or weights can be modularized, you might load only the parts needed for a specific request or user.
- **On-Demand Pipeline Steps**: Rather than processing the entire data pipeline for each request, you only execute the steps relevant to the query.

3.4.4 Implementing Caching in RESTful APIs

Below is a simplified Python Flask example:

```
from flask import Flask, request, jsonify
import functools
import time

app = Flask(__name__)

# A simple in-memory cache (not recommended for
production)
cache = {}

def cached(func):
    @functools.wraps(func)
    def wrapper(*args, **kwargs):
```

```python
        key = str(args) + str(kwargs)
        if key in cache:
            return cache[key]
        result = func(*args, **kwargs)
        cache[key] = result
        return result
    return wrapper

@cached
def run_inference(input_data):
    # Simulate a heavy computation
    time.sleep(2)
    return {"prediction": "cat"}

@app.route('/predict', methods=['POST'])
def predict():
    data = request.get_json()
    result = run_inference(data)
    return jsonify(result)

if __name__ == '__main__':
    app.run()
```

- **Explanation**:

    - The @cached decorator stores the output of run_inference in a dictionary.
    - Subsequent requests with the same input data return the cached result immediately.
    - In production, you'd use a more robust caching solution like Redis, Memcached, or a dedicated microservice.

- **Trade-Offs**:

    - **Memory Usage**: Caching can consume significant memory if many unique inputs are encountered.
    - **Cache Invalidation**: If the model or data changes, cached results may become stale.

3.5 Conclusion and What's Next

In this chapter, we explored **four powerful techniques** for optimizing machine learning models and their serving patterns:

1. **Quantization**: Reducing numerical precision to speed up arithmetic and lower memory usage.
2. **Pruning**: Removing redundant or insignificant weights and neurons to shrink model size and potentially improve inference speed.
3. **Knowledge Distillation**: Training a smaller student model to replicate the performance of a larger teacher model.
4. **Caching and Lazy Loading**: Streamlining data access and inference paths to cut down on redundant computations and reduce latency.

Each of these techniques offers its own **set of benefits** and **trade-offs**. Quantization and pruning directly modify the model, potentially affecting accuracy. Knowledge distillation requires an additional training process but often results in a more compact yet capable model. Caching primarily tackles performance at the **system** or **API** level and involves considerations like cache storage and invalidation.

Next Steps: In **Chapter 4**, we'll delve into the **tools and frameworks** that can help you implement these optimizations seamlessly. From specialized GPU inference engines like **TensorRT** to cross-framework solutions like **ONNX Runtime** and compiler-based approaches like **Apache TVM**, we'll show you how to integrate these tools into your workflow and harness hardware-specific optimizations for maximum speed and efficiency.

Key Takeaways

1. **Quantization**: Great for reducing compute and memory load; watch out for accuracy drop, especially

if post-training quantization is used without calibration.

2. **Pruning**: Focus on removing unimportant parameters; structured pruning is often easier to accelerate on typical hardware.

3. **Knowledge Distillation**: Ideal for obtaining a small, efficient model without losing most of the original accuracy; requires an additional training phase.

4. **Caching and Lazy Loading**: Target overall system performance by avoiding repeated computations; be mindful of cache invalidation and memory overhead.

5. **Holistic Approach**: Combine these techniques where appropriate. For example, you might prune your model, then quantize it, and further speed up your API responses with caching for a multi-pronged optimization strategy.

Armed with this knowledge, you're now ready to explore how **industry-grade tools** can streamline your optimization efforts —making it simpler to integrate these best practices into your production pipelines.

Chapter 4: Tools and Frameworks

In the previous chapters, we explored the motivations behind model optimization, where it fits in the deployment lifecycle, and the various techniques—quantization, pruning, knowledge distillation, and caching—that can help us achieve better performance. However, effectively implementing these techniques often requires specialized **tools and frameworks** that can automate or streamline many of the underlying processes.

In this chapter, we dive into four key solutions that have become industry standards for optimizing and deploying models across different hardware backends:

1. **TensorRT** – NVIDIA's high-performance deep learning inference optimizer for GPUs.
2. **ONNX Runtime** – A cross-platform engine that leverages the ONNX format for interoperability and optimization.
3. **TensorFlow Lite** – A lightweight runtime designed for mobile and edge deployments.
4. **Apache TVM** – A compiler stack that automatically generates optimized code for multiple hardware backends.

By the end of this chapter, you will have a clearer idea of how to choose the right tool for your specific scenario and how to integrate these frameworks into your existing workflows.

4.1 TensorRT

4.1.1 Overview and Use Cases

TensorRT is an SDK (Software Development Kit) developed by NVIDIA to optimize deep learning inference on NVIDIA

GPUs. It takes your trained model—usually in formats like TensorFlow, ONNX, or PyTorch (via exported ONNX)—and converts it into a highly optimized runtime engine that can run faster on NVIDIA hardware.

- **Key Features**:
  - **Layer Fusion**: Combines multiple operations into a single GPU kernel to reduce memory bandwidth overhead.
  - **Mixed-Precision Support**: Supports FP32, FP16, and INT8 precision, automatically applying lower precision where beneficial.
  - **Automatic Optimizations**: Discovers the best execution path, scheduling, and kernel choices based on the GPU architecture.
- **Use Cases**:
  - **High-Throughput Inference**: Ideal for data centers or enterprise applications needing to serve large numbers of requests concurrently.
  - **Latency-Critical Services**: Real-time systems —like recommendation engines or live video analytics—benefit from the significant speedups that TensorRT can offer.
  - **Production-Grade Deployments**: TensorRT includes robust APIs and integration options for deploying on-premises or in cloud environments that utilize NVIDIA GPUs.

4.1.2 Example: Optimizing a Deep Learning Model for GPU Inference

Below is a simplified workflow illustrating how one might convert a PyTorch model to ONNX, then optimize it using TensorRT.

1. **Export a PyTorch Model to ONNX**

```
import torch
import torchvision.models as models
```

```
model =
models.resnet50(pretrained=True).eval()

# Dummy input to define input shape
dummy_input = torch.randn(1, 3, 224, 224)

# Export to ONNX
torch.onnx.export(
    model,
    dummy_input,
    "resnet50.onnx",
    input_names=["input"],
    output_names=["output"],
    opset_version=11
)
```

2. Use TensorRT's Command-Line Tool (trtexec)
   Assuming you have TensorRT installed, the `trtexec`
   tool can convert your ONNX model into an optimized
   TensorRT engine:

```
trtexec --onnx=resnet50.onnx \
        --saveEngine=resnet50_trt.engine \
        --fp16  # Enable FP16 precision if
your GPU supports it
```

3. **Run Inference with TensorRT Python API**

```
import tensorrt as trt
import pycuda.driver as cuda
import pycuda.autoinit
import numpy as np

# Load the engine
TRT_LOGGER = trt.Logger(trt.Logger.WARNING)
with open("resnet50_trt.engine", "rb") as f,
trt.Runtime(TRT_LOGGER) as runtime:
    engine =
runtime.deserialize_cuda_engine(f.read())

# Create execution context
context = engine.create_execution_context()

# Prepare input and output buffers
input_shape = (1, 3, 224, 224)
host_input =
np.random.randn(*input_shape).astype(np.floa
t32).ravel()
host_output = np.empty((1, 1000),
dtype=np.float32)  # For ImageNet
classification with 1000 classes
```

```
# Allocate device memory
d_input = cuda.mem_alloc(host_input.nbytes)
d_output =
cuda.mem_alloc(host_output.nbytes)

# Transfer input data to device
cuda.memcpy_htod(d_input, host_input)

# Execute inference
context.execute_v2([int(d_input),
int(d_output)])

# Copy predictions back to host
cuda.memcpy_dtoh(host_output, d_output)

# Process output
predictions = np.reshape(host_output, (1,
1000))
print("Top-5 predictions:",
np.argsort(predictions, axis=1)[..., -5:])
```

This pipeline demonstrates how to load an optimized TensorRT engine and run inference at high speed on an NVIDIA GPU.

4. **Performance Gains**

- By enabling FP16 or INT8 (with calibration), you can often achieve significant speedups (2x–5x or more) compared to standard FP32 inference.
- Always test your accuracy, as lower precision can introduce small numerical differences.

4.2 ONNX Runtime

4.2.1 Why ONNX for Cross-Framework Optimization?

ONNX (Open Neural Network Exchange) is an open format originally developed by Facebook (Meta) and Microsoft. It serves as a common representation for machine learning models across various frameworks like PyTorch, TensorFlow, and scikit-learn.

The **ONNX Runtime** is a high-performance inference engine that executes ONNX models with optimizations for a range of hardware backends—CPUs, GPUs, and more specialized accelerators.

- **Key Benefits**:
  - **Interoperability**: Train in PyTorch, export to ONNX, and deploy with ONNX Runtime anywhere.
  - **Automatic Graph Optimizations**: ONNX Runtime applies its own set of transformations (e.g., operator fusion) to speed up inference.
  - **Hardware Plugins**: Supports different execution providers—like CPU (default), CUDA for NVIDIA GPUs, DirectML on Windows, etc.

4.2.2 Hands-On: Converting a PyTorch Model to ONNX and Optimizing It

1. **Export Model to ONNX**
   (Similar to the example in the TensorRT section.)

```
import torch
import torchvision.models as models

model =
models.mobilenet_v2(pretrained=True).eval()
dummy_input = torch.randn(1, 3, 224, 224)
torch.onnx.export(model, dummy_input,
"mobilenet_v2.onnx", opset_version=11)
```

2. Install ONNX Runtime

```
pip install onnxruntime
```

3. Run Inference with ONNX Runtime

```
import onnxruntime as ort
import numpy as np

# Create an inference session
session =
ort.InferenceSession("mobilenet_v2.onnx",
providers=["CPUExecutionProvider"])
```

```
# Prepare inputs
input_data = np.random.randn(1, 3, 224,
224).astype(np.float32)
inputs = {session.get_inputs()[0].name:
input_data}

# Inference
outputs = session.run(None, inputs)
predictions = outputs[0]
print("Predictions shape:",
predictions.shape)
```

4. **Hardware Acceleration and Optimization**

- **Execution Providers**: For GPU acceleration, install `onnxruntime-gpu` and set `providers=["CUDAExecutionProvider"]`.

- **Graph Optimizations**: ONNX Runtime automatically fuses certain operations at runtime. You can enable higher optimization levels by specifying:

```
session_options = ort.SessionOptions()
session_options.graph_optimization_lev
el =
ort.GraphOptimizationLevel.ORT_ENABLE_
ALL
session =
ort.InferenceSession("mobilenet_v2.onn
x", sess_options=session_options)
```

- **Quantization**: ONNX Runtime supports post-training quantization via **onnxruntime.quantization**. You can quantize your floating-point model into INT8 for further speedup on compatible hardware.

The result is a highly portable, optimized model that can be deployed across a variety of environments with minimal changes to your code.

4.3 TensorFlow Lite

4.3.1 Optimizing for Mobile and Edge Devices

TensorFlow Lite (TFLite) is a lightweight version of TensorFlow specifically designed for mobile and embedded devices. It offers a small footprint, fast initialization, and optimizations tailored to **ARM CPUs**, **DSPs**, and **NPUs** commonly found in smartphones and IoT devices.

- **Why TensorFlow Lite?**
  - **Low Latency**: Executes models quickly, even on resource-constrained hardware.
  - **Reduced Model Size**: Provides built-in tools for quantization and pruning, targeting lower-precision data types.
  - **Broad Hardware Support**: Runtimes for Android, iOS, and various embedded platforms (e.g., Raspberry Pi, microcontrollers).

4.3.2 Example: Deploying a TFLite Model on an Android App

1. **Convert a TensorFlow Model to TFLite**

```
import tensorflow as tf

# Suppose you have a trained Keras model
model =
tf.keras.applications.MobileNetV2(weights='i
magenet')

# Convert to TFLite
converter =
tf.lite.TFLiteConverter.from_keras_model(mod
el)
converter.optimizations =
[tf.lite.Optimize.DEFAULT]  # Enable
optimizations (quantization, etc.)
tflite_model = converter.convert()

# Save the converted model
with open("mobilenet_v2.tflite", "wb") as f:
    f.write(tflite_model)
```

2. Add the TFLite Model to your Android Project

- Copy `mobilenet_v2.tflite` into your app's `assets` folder.

- Include the TensorFlow Lite library in your `build.gradle`:

```
implementation
'org.tensorflow:tensorflow-lite:2.9.0'
```

3. Load and Run Inference on Android

```
import org.tensorflow.lite.Interpreter;
import
android.content.res.AssetFileDescriptor;
import java.io.FileInputStream;
import java.nio.MappedByteBuffer;
import java.nio.channels.FileChannel;

private MappedByteBuffer
loadModelFile(String modelPath) throws
IOException {
    AssetFileDescriptor fileDescriptor =
getAssets().openFd(modelPath);
    FileInputStream inputStream = new
FileInputStream(fileDescriptor.getFileDescri
ptor());
    FileChannel fileChannel =
inputStream.getChannel();
    long startOffset =
fileDescriptor.getStartOffset();
    long declaredLength =
fileDescriptor.getDeclaredLength();
    return
fileChannel.map(FileChannel.MapMode.READ_ONL
Y, startOffset, declaredLength);
}

private float[][] runInference(Bitmap image)
{
    try {
        MappedByteBuffer modelBuffer =
loadModelFile("mobilenet_v2.tflite");
        Interpreter tflite = new
Interpreter(modelBuffer);

        // Preprocess the image into a float
input
        float[][][][] input =
convertBitmapToFloatInput(image);

        // Allocate output
```

```java
        float[][] output = new float[1]
[1000]; // e.g., 1000 classes for ImageNet
        tflite.run(input, output);

        return output;
    } catch (IOException e) {
        e.printStackTrace();
        return null;
    }
}
```

- **Explanation**:
  - Load the `.tflite` file from the assets folder.
  - Create an `Interpreter` instance.
  - Preprocess the image to match the model's input shape and range.
  - Run inference and retrieve the predictions.

4. **Optimizations and Advanced Features**

   - **GPU Delegate**: TFLite provides a GPU delegate to accelerate inference on mobile GPUs.
     - **NNAPI Delegate**: Uses Android's Neural Networks API for hardware-accelerated inference when available.
     - **Quantized Models**: Use `converter.target_spec.supported_ops = [tf.lite.OpsSet.TFLITE_BUILTINS_INT8]` to fully quantize your model for even smaller size and faster inference (with a potential accuracy trade-off).

TensorFlow Lite thus enables developers to deploy advanced machine learning applications—like image classification, object detection, or speech recognition—on mobile and edge devices with efficient performance and minimal footprint.

4.4 Apache TVM

4.4.1 Compilation for Multiple Hardware Backends

Apache TVM (Tensor Virtual Machine) is an open-source deep learning compiler stack that can take a high-level model representation—like PyTorch, TensorFlow, or ONNX—and **compile it down** to highly optimized machine code for a variety of backends (e.g., CPUs, GPUs, specialized accelerators like ARM Mali GPUs, Intel CPUs, NVIDIA GPUs, and more).

- **Key Advantages**:
    - **Performance Portability**: Once you define a model in a supported front-end, TVM can generate optimized code for different architectures.
    - **Auto-Tuning**: TVM includes an auto-scheduler that can search for the best kernel implementations.
    - **Custom Operators**: You can extend TVM with specialized kernels, making it suitable for cutting-edge research and specialized hardware.

4.4.2 Step-by-Step: Using TVM to Optimize a Model for ARM Processors

1. **Install TVM**

    - TVM can be installed from source or via pip, though the source installation is often recommended to get the latest features.

    - Make sure you have LLVM, CMake, and other dependencies:

    ```
    git clone --recursive
    https://github.com/apache/tvm.git
    cd tvm
    mkdir build
    cp cmake/config.cmake build
    ```

```
# Edit build/config.cmake to enable
desired features (e.g., ARM support)
cd build
cmake ..
make -j4
```

- Add `python/tvm` to your PYTHONPATH.

2. Import a Model (e.g. ONNX)

```
import onnx
import tvm
from tvm import relay

# Load an ONNX model
onnx_model = onnx.load("resnet50.onnx")

# Convert ONNX model to a Relay graph
shape_dict = {"input": (1, 3, 224, 224)}
mod, params =
relay.frontend.from_onnx(onnx_model,
shape_dict)
```

3. Define the Target Hardware

```
# Example target for ARM CPU
target = tvm.target.Target("llvm -
mtriple=armv7l-linux-gnueabihf")
# If optimizing for a Raspberry Pi, you
might specify more details about the CPU.
```

4. Build and Optimize with TVM

```
with tvm.transform.PassContext(opt_level=3):
    lib = relay.build(mod, target=target,
params=params)
```

- Explanation:
  - `opt_level=3` applies advanced optimizations like operator fusion and layout transformations.

5. **Auto-Tuning** *(Optional but recommended for better performance)*

- TVM's **AutoTVM** or **Ansor** can profile different operator implementations and search for the fastest configuration.

- This step can significantly improve performance on specialized hardware.

6. **Deploy the Model**

```
import numpy as np
from tvm.contrib import graph_executor

dev = tvm.cpu()  # For local testing; on the
actual ARM device, you might use a remote
RPC
module =
graph_executor.GraphModule(lib["default"]
(dev))

# Run inference
input_data = np.random.randn(1, 3, 224,
224).astype("float32")
module.set_input("input", input_data)
module.run()
output = module.get_output(0).asnumpy()
print("Output shape:", output.shape)
```

TVM's main strength lies in its **compiler-based approach**: it analyzes your model's computational graph at a low level, optimizes it specifically for the target device, and generates efficient code. This can yield substantial performance boosts, especially if you take the time to fine-tune and auto-schedule.

4.5 Choosing the Right Tool

Each of the tools and frameworks discussed in this chapter serves a different set of use cases:

- **TensorRT**:
  - **Best for**: NVIDIA GPUs, high-throughput data center or edge GPU inference.
  - **Advantages**: Automatic mixed-precision, layer fusion, tight integration with NVIDIA ecosystem.
  - **Drawbacks**: Limited to NVIDIA hardware, requires ONNX conversion or TensorFlow-to-TensorRT steps.
- **ONNX Runtime**:

- **Best for**: Cross-platform deployment (CPU, GPU, specialized accelerators), easy interoperability between PyTorch, TensorFlow, etc.
- **Advantages**: One format (ONNX) for many frameworks; built-in optimizations and quantization.
- **Drawbacks**: Some specialized ops may not be fully supported, requiring custom workarounds.

- **TensorFlow Lite**:

  - **Best for**: Mobile and IoT devices, especially Android/iOS.
  - **Advantages**: Minimal runtime size, built-in GPU/NNAPI delegates, straightforward to integrate into native mobile apps.
  - **Drawbacks**: Primarily for inference on resource-constrained devices; advanced model architectures may require additional custom ops.

- **Apache TVM**:

  - **Best for**: Users who need performance portability across diverse hardware (CPUs, GPUs, ARM, etc.).
  - **Advantages**: Compiler-based approach that can yield significant performance gains; auto-tuning.
  - **Drawbacks**: Steeper learning curve; advanced configuration often required.

In many production environments, teams use **multiple** tools. For instance, you might develop a model in PyTorch, export it to ONNX, then use TensorRT for GPU servers and TensorFlow Lite for mobile apps. Or, you might rely on Apache TVM for specialized hardware deployments while using ONNX Runtime for a quick cross-platform solution.

4.6 Conclusion and Next Steps

Optimizing a machine learning model goes beyond just tweaking parameters; it often requires leveraging specialized **software stacks** to unlock the full potential of modern hardware. TensorRT, ONNX Runtime, TensorFlow Lite, and Apache TVM each tackle the optimization challenge from different angles, offering unique features and ecosystems for model acceleration.

- **TensorRT**: High-performance GPU inference on NVIDIA hardware.
- **ONNX Runtime**: Cross-platform engine supporting CPU, GPU, and specialized devices.
- **TensorFlow Lite**: Tailored for mobile and edge environments, with a tiny footprint.
- **Apache TVM**: A universal compiler approach for maximum flexibility across diverse backends.

Next Steps: In **Chapter 5**, we'll delve deeper into **hardware-specific optimizations**. We'll look at the nuances of deploying on CPUs vs. GPUs vs. TPUs, explore profiling techniques, and walk through examples of how to tailor your model to the strengths and limitations of each hardware architecture. This knowledge will help you make even more informed decisions about which tool or framework to use— and how to configure it—for optimal performance in your unique deployment scenario.

Key Takeaways

1. **Tools and Frameworks Are Essential**

   - Effective optimization often hinges on specialized software that applies low-level optimizations and hardware-specific tweaks automatically.

2. **TensorRT for NVIDIA GPUs**

- Fast, powerful, and well-integrated in the NVIDIA ecosystem, but hardware-limited.

3. **ONNX Runtime for Interoperability**

   - A universal execution engine that works across platforms and frameworks, with strong built-in optimization features.

4. **TensorFlow Lite for Mobile and Edge**

   - Offers a slim runtime optimized for limited-resource devices, with support for hardware accelerators on mobile.

5. **Apache TVM for Compiler-Based Optimization**

   - Provides a high degree of performance portability and customization through auto-tuning and graph compilation.

6. **Mix and Match**

   - Large-scale applications may use more than one tool to cover different deployment scenarios (e.g., GPUs in the cloud and microcontrollers at the edge).

With an understanding of these frameworks, you're better positioned to choose the right tool for your workflow and hardware environment, ensuring your models achieve **peak performance** once deployed.

Chapter 5: Hardware-Specific Optimization

The performance of a machine learning model is not solely determined by the model architecture or the algorithmic optimizations applied—**the underlying hardware** also plays a significant role. Different hardware architectures (e.g., CPUs, GPUs, and TPUs) are optimized for different types of workloads. Understanding how these architectures work can help you tailor your model and deployment strategy to achieve maximum efficiency and throughput.

In this chapter, we explore:

1. **CPU vs. GPU vs. TPU** – How each hardware type impacts model performance and optimization strategies.
2. **Strategies for Hardware-Aware Optimization** – Practical ways to adapt your models to different computing environments.
3. **Example: Profiling and Optimizing a Model for NVIDIA GPUs** – A hands-on demonstration showing how to identify bottlenecks and boost performance for GPU-based deployments.

By the end, you'll have a clear understanding of how to choose and optimize for the hardware that best suits your use case—whether you're running on commodity CPUs, enterprise-grade GPUs, or specialized accelerators like TPUs.

5.1 CPU vs. GPU vs. TPU: How Hardware Impacts Optimization

5.1.1 CPU (Central Processing Unit)

CPUs are general-purpose processors designed to handle a wide variety of tasks. They typically have fewer cores (e.g., 4 to 64 in most server environments) but run at higher clock speeds and exhibit strong single-threaded performance. CPUs also have a relatively large cache hierarchy (L1, L2, L3) to speed up memory access for sequential tasks.

- **Strengths**:
    - **Versatility**: Great for diverse workloads (data preprocessing, system orchestration, smaller models).
    - **Low Memory Footprint**: Well-suited for models that aren't very large or for batch processing in environments where memory is constrained.
    - **Mature Ecosystem**: Many libraries (e.g., Intel MKL, oneDNN) offer CPU-optimized math routines.
- **Drawbacks**:
    - **Lower Parallel Throughput**: Not as efficient as GPUs for highly parallel tasks (such as deep neural network training or large-scale inference).
    - **Scaling**: To achieve massive throughput, you often need large CPU clusters, which can be expensive.
- **Typical Use Cases**:
    - **Edge and On-Premises**: When GPU access is limited or cost-prohibitive.
    - **Sparse or Small Models**: Certain smaller or classical ML models may run just as fast on CPUs.
    - **Microservices**: Model serving systems that handle relatively low throughput or benefit from CPU-only containers (easy to deploy and scale horizontally).

5.1.2 GPU (Graphics Processing Unit)

GPUs are specialized hardware originally designed for rendering graphics, which is inherently a parallel task. Over time, GPUs have become the workhorse for training and serving deep learning models because they contain thousands of lightweight cores capable of performing matrix and vector operations in parallel.

- **Strengths**:
    - **Massive Parallelism**: Ideal for matrix-heavy operations like those in convolutional neural networks and Transformers.
    - **High Throughput**: Typically achieve orders-of-magnitude speedups for large batches of data.
    - **Broad Ecosystem**: Frameworks like TensorFlow, PyTorch, CUDA libraries, and vendor-specific optimizers (e.g., NVIDIA TensorRT) provide robust GPU support.
- **Drawbacks**:
    - **Energy and Heat**: GPUs consume more power and generate more heat, which can lead to higher operational costs.
    - **Cost**: High-performance GPUs are expensive, both in acquisition and in cloud rental fees (per-hour cost).
    - **Memory Limitations**: GPUs often have less memory than a CPU server (though modern GPUs can have 24GB+), which can limit batch sizes and model size.
- **Typical Use Cases**:
    - **Deep Neural Network Training**: CNNs, RNNs, Transformers—all benefit from massive parallelism.
    - **Real-Time Inference**: When you need to handle thousands or millions of inferences per second at low latency.

- **Data Center Scale**: Large-scale deployments with high concurrency.

5.1.3 TPU (Tensor Processing Unit)

TPUs are custom-built accelerators created by Google specifically for machine learning tasks, particularly those involving TensorFlow. They are designed to accelerate linear algebra operations, such as matrix multiplications, at even greater scales and efficiencies than general-purpose GPUs—especially for **highly structured** neural network workloads (e.g., large-scale training of Transformers).

- **Strengths**:

  - **Highly Specialized**: Optimized for matrix multiplication and convolution-like operations.
  - **Scalability**: TPUs can be grouped into "pods," offering thousands of cores for very large-scale training.
  - **Integration with Google Cloud**: Easy to spin up on Google Cloud Platform for large training jobs.
- **Drawbacks**:

  - **Availability**: Primarily available through Google Cloud (though there are limited on-prem TPU offerings).
  - **Flexibility**: Best leveraged within the TensorFlow ecosystem—PyTorch has TPU support via XLA, but the ecosystem is more limited.
  - **Cost Model**: Pricing structures can be steep for large TPU pods.
- **Typical Use Cases**:

  - **Large-Scale Deep Learning**: Training massive language models, image classification networks, or any large-scale workload using TensorFlow.

- **Research**: Institutions doing cutting-edge AI research requiring HPC-level compute.
- **High-Volume Inference**: Serving production workloads on Cloud TPU, though more common for training than inference.

5.2 Strategies for Hardware-Aware Optimization

Now that we've examined the characteristics of CPUs, GPUs, and TPUs, let's delve into **hardware-aware** optimization strategies—techniques that specifically cater to the strengths and limitations of each hardware type.

5.2.1 CPU Optimization Strategies

1. **Vectorized Libraries**

   - Utilize libraries like **Intel MKL**, **OpenBLAS**, or **oneDNN** (Deep Neural Network library) which provide vectorized math kernels optimized for x86 or ARM CPUs.

2. **Multi-Threading and Parallelization**

   - Enable parallelism where possible (e.g., using OpenMP or framework-level parallelization) to fully utilize the CPU's cores.

3. **Batch Sizing**

   - For CPU-based inference, moderate batching can help amortize overhead. However, extremely large batches may diminish performance due to cache misses and context switching.

4. **Low-Precision Inference**

   - Some modern CPUs support **AVX2** or **AVX-512** vector instructions for INT8 or BF16 operations, offering speedups similar to GPU-based quantization benefits.

5. **Compiler Optimizations**

- Use advanced compiler flags (`-march=native -O3`) and Link Time Optimization (LTO) to squeeze out additional performance from the CPU.

5.2.2 GPU Optimization Strategies

1. **Efficient Memory Usage**

- **Coalesced Access**: Organize data to maximize memory bandwidth usage.
- **Pinned Memory**: For frequent host-device transfers, pinned (page-locked) memory can reduce transfer overhead.

2. **Kernel Fusion**

- Tools like **TensorRT**, **CuDNN**, and **XLA (Accelerated Linear Algebra)** can fuse multiple operations into a single kernel, reducing the overhead of kernel launches.

3. **Mixed Precision**

- **FP16** or **BF16** training and inference can significantly boost throughput without large accuracy penalties, particularly on GPUs with Tensor Cores (e.g., NVIDIA Volta, Turing, Ampere architectures).

4. **Batching and Streaming**

- Use appropriate batch sizes to keep GPU cores busy. However, for real-time workloads, smaller batches might reduce latency.
- **Asynchronous execution** can overlap data transfers and computation to maximize GPU utilization.

5. **Profiling and Tuning**

- **NVIDIA Nsight Systems**, **Nsight Compute**, or **CUDA Profiler** can help identify hotspots.

- Adjust launch parameters (block size, grid size) if you write custom CUDA kernels.

5.2.3 TPU Optimization Strategies

1. **XLA Compiler**

    - TensorFlow's **XLA** (Accelerated Linear Algebra) compiler is crucial for compiling models to run efficiently on TPUs.
    - Use the `jit_compile=True` or `tf.function` decorators in TensorFlow 2.x to let XLA optimize your graph.

2. **Batching**

    - TPUs thrive on larger batch sizes because they are designed for high throughput.
    - However, monitor memory usage; going too large can lead to out-of-memory errors.

3. **Precision Modes**

    - TPUs support **bfloat16** (BF16) at the hardware level. BF16 offers the same dynamic range as FP32 but uses half the bits for the significand —leading to speedups without significantly hurting accuracy.

4. **TPU-Specific Operations**

    - Certain ops (like LSTM variants, or non-standard layers) might not be natively supported on TPUs.
    - Stick to common deep learning building blocks (convolutions, matrix multiplications, batch norm) for best performance.

5. **Data Pipeline Optimization**

    - Ensure that your input pipeline (e.g., using `tf.data`) can keep up with the TPU's throughput.

- Preprocessing or data augmentation steps might become the bottleneck if not carefully managed.

5.3 Example: Profiling and Optimizing a Model for NVIDIA GPUs

To illustrate how to put these principles into practice, let's walk through an **end-to-end workflow** for profiling and optimizing a model specifically for NVIDIA GPUs. We'll use a PyTorch-based example, but similar principles apply to TensorFlow or other frameworks.

5.3.1 Step 1: Baseline Training and Inference

1. **Load a Model**

```
import torch
import torchvision.models as models

device = torch.device("cuda" if
torch.cuda.is_available() else "cpu")
model =
models.resnet50(pretrained=True).to(device)
model.eval()
```

2. Run a baseline inference loop

```
import time
import numpy as np

dummy_input = torch.randn(32, 3, 224,
224).to(device)
N = 50  # Number of iterations

start_time = time.time()
with torch.no_grad():
    for _ in range(N):
        _ = model(dummy_input)
baseline_time = time.time() - start_time

print(f"Baseline Inference Time for {N}
iterations: {baseline_time:.4f}s")
```

3. **Observe Results**

- You get a baseline throughput or latency figure (e.g., X ms per inference for a batch of 32).

5.3.2 Step 2: Profiling with NVIDIA Tools

Use **Nsight Systems** or **Nsight Compute** to identify performance bottlenecks. For a quick command-line approach, you can also use **CUDA's built-in profiler**:

```
nvprof python baseline_inference.py
```

- **Key Metrics**:
  - **GPU Utilization**: How busy is the GPU?
  - **Kernel Execution Time**: Which operations (kernels) consume the most time?
  - **Memory Throughput**: Are we saturating memory bandwidth?
  - **PCIe Transfer**: Are repeated host-to-device data transfers a bottleneck?

5.3.3 Step 3: Apply Mixed Precision

Mixed-precision can drastically speed up inference if the GPU supports **Tensor Cores** (e.g., NVIDIA T4, V100, A100). In PyTorch, you can use the `torch.cuda.amp` (Automatic Mixed Precision) API:

```
from torch.cuda.amp import autocast

model.half().to(device)  # Convert weights to FP16

with torch.no_grad(), autocast():
    start_time = time.time()
    for _ in range(N):
        _ = model(dummy_input.half())  # Input
also in FP16
    mixed_precision_time = time.time() -
start_time

print(f"Mixed Precision Inference Time:
{mixed_precision_time:.4f}s")
```

- **Watch Out**: Some layers (e.g., batch norm) may need special handling, though PyTorch has improved compatibility over time.

- **Accuracy Check**: Verify that going from FP32 to FP16 doesn't degrade accuracy beyond acceptable limits.

5.3.4 Step 4: Use TensorRT or Other Accelerators

If further optimization is needed:

1. **Export the Model to ONNX**

```
dummy_input = torch.randn(32, 3, 224,
224).to(device)
torch.onnx.export(model.float().cpu(),   #
Convert back to FP32
                    dummy_input.cpu(),
                    "resnet50.onnx",
                    opset_version=11)
```

2. **Run TensorRT Optimization** (as demonstrated in Chapter 4)

```
trtexec --onnx=resnet50.onnx \
          --saveEngine=resnet50_fp16.engine \
          --fp16 \
          --maxBatch=32
```

3. **Deploy** the `.engine` file in a production environment or embed it in your application code using TensorRT's Python or C++ APIs.

5.3.5 Step 5: Measure and Compare

- **Final Check**: Compare baseline (FP32 in PyTorch) vs. mixed-precision vs. TensorRT engine.
- **Metrics to Record**:
    - Inference latency per batch.
    - Throughput (inferences per second).
    - Memory usage and GPU utilization.
    - Accuracy or other relevant performance metrics (especially if quantization or half-precision is used).

By systematically profiling at each step and applying the appropriate hardware-specific optimizations, you can often see **2x, 4x, or even greater** performance gains—without drastically altering your model's architecture or code.

5.4 Conclusion

Hardware plays a pivotal role in determining how—and how well—your machine learning models perform in production. CPUs, GPUs, and TPUs each bring unique strengths and challenges:

- **CPUs** offer flexibility and a mature ecosystem but can struggle with large-scale parallel workloads.
- **GPUs** excel at deep learning tasks thanks to massive parallelism, but come with higher costs and specific data layout considerations.
- **TPUs** specialize in large-scale TensorFlow-based workloads, achieving impressive results in training and inference but with more limited ecosystem flexibility.

Hardware-aware optimization ensures you capitalize on each architecture's strengths. Whether you're vectorizing operations for a CPU, leveraging Tensor Cores on a GPU, or scaling up via TPU pods, being mindful of memory access patterns, batching, precision modes, and specialized libraries can yield substantial performance benefits.

Next Steps: In **Chapter 6**, we'll look at **scaling and monitoring** your machine learning services. Once your model is optimized for the hardware, you'll need robust strategies for horizontal or vertical scaling, load balancing, and real-time performance monitoring to keep everything running smoothly at scale.

Key Takeaways

1. **Hardware Matters**: CPU vs. GPU vs. TPU have fundamentally different architectures; choose based on your workload and cost constraints.

2. **CPU Optimization**: Vectorized libraries, multi-threading, and compiler optimizations can boost performance for smaller or more flexible workloads.
3. **GPU Optimization**: Mixed precision, kernel fusion, and batching strategies are essential for unleashing full GPU parallelism.
4. **TPU Optimization**: Leverage bfloat16 and the XLA compiler for large-scale TensorFlow workloads.
5. **Profiling Is Essential**: Always profile your model to identify bottlenecks and apply targeted optimizations.
6. **Iterative Process**: Optimization is not a one-time task; it's a cycle of measurement, analysis, and improvement as hardware, software frameworks, and user demands evolve.

With a deep understanding of hardware-specific strategies, you are well-prepared to deploy highly efficient AI models that meet your performance, latency, and cost targets—no matter which computing environment you operate in.

Chapter 6: Scaling and Monitoring

Optimizing the performance of your machine learning models is only one piece of the puzzle. Once you've refined your models to be as resource-efficient and responsive as possible, the question becomes: **How do you handle growth in demand, unpredictable traffic spikes, and ongoing performance management?** This is where **scaling** and **monitoring** come into play.

In this chapter, we explore:

1. **Scaling Models in Production** – Strategies for increasing capacity to handle higher volumes of inference requests.
2. **Monitoring Performance** – Setting up a robust infrastructure to keep tabs on latency, throughput, error rates, and more.

By the end of this chapter, you will understand how to **grow** your serving infrastructure in a sustainable way and **maintain** your models' performance over time—even in the face of evolving data distributions, user traffic patterns, and hardware configurations.

6.1 Scaling Models in Production

Model optimization helps ensure that each instance of your model is as efficient as possible. However, there are limits to how far you can optimize a single node or container. At some point—especially when dealing with high-traffic applications—you'll need to scale horizontally or vertically (or both) to meet performance requirements.

6.1.1 Horizontal vs. Vertical Scaling

1. **Horizontal Scaling** (Scaling Out)

- **Definition**: Adding more instances of your service (e.g., more servers, containers, or pods) to distribute the load.
- **Benefits**:
  - Flexible resource allocation—you can add or remove instances to match traffic patterns.
  - Reduces the risk of a single point of failure; if one instance goes down, others can continue serving requests.
- **Drawbacks**:
  - More complex orchestration—load balancers, container orchestrators (Kubernetes, Docker Swarm), or serverless frameworks.
  - Potentially higher network overhead if request routing isn't optimized.

2. **Vertical Scaling** (Scaling Up)

- **Definition**: Increasing the resources (CPU cores, GPU memory, RAM) on a single machine or VM.
- **Benefits**:
  - Simpler architecture—no need for complex load balancing or distribution logic.
  - Often straightforward if you're renting compute instances in the cloud (e.g., upgrading from a small VM to a larger one).
- **Drawbacks**:
  - There's an upper hardware limit. Eventually, adding more resources to a single machine yields diminishing returns.
  - Can be costly, and a single machine still represents a single point of failure.

Many production systems use a **hybrid approach**—they optimize each node (vertical scaling to an extent) and then replicate those nodes (horizontal scaling) behind a load balancer to handle larger total throughput.

6.1.2 Load Balancing and Autoscaling Strategies

1. **Round-Robin Load Balancing**

   - Requests are distributed sequentially across multiple instances.
   - Easy to set up but doesn't account for differences in instance performance or resource utilization.

2. **Least-Connections / Least-Load**

   - Directs traffic to the instance with the fewest active connections or lowest utilization.
   - More sophisticated, potentially more efficient for heterogeneous clusters.

3. **Autoscaling**

   - **CPU/GPU Utilization Metrics**: Scale up when average CPU or GPU usage exceeds a threshold (e.g., 70%) for a sustained period. Scale down when usage drops below a lower threshold.
   - **Custom Application Metrics**: Scale based on domain-specific metrics, such as inference latency, queue depth, or request throughput.
   - **Serverless Inference**: Some cloud providers offer fully managed autoscaling for containerized or function-based inference endpoints (e.g., AWS Lambda, Google Cloud Run). This approach can reduce operational overhead but may incur higher per-inference costs.

Autoscaling is particularly important for machine learning deployments, as traffic can be **bursty**—for instance, an e-commerce recommendation service might see large spikes during holiday sales. With proper autoscaling, you can dynamically add resources to handle peak loads and scale back during quieter periods.

6.1.3 Practical Considerations for Scaling

- **Stateful vs. Stateless**: Machine learning inference services are often stateless—you pass an input, get an output—making them easier to scale horizontally. Stateful services that maintain a session or context (e.g., conversation context in chatbots) may require additional synchronization or data sharing.
- **Cascading Models**: Some architectures involve multiple models in a pipeline (e.g., a coarse model followed by a refined model). Ensuring each stage is scaled appropriately to avoid bottlenecks is crucial.
- **Caching**: Revisit caching strategies (Chapter 3.4) to reduce redundant computations. This becomes especially important at scale—caching high-frequency queries or intermediate results can dramatically lower the load on downstream models.

6.2 Monitoring Performance

Once you've scaled your infrastructure, the next challenge is **maintaining visibility** into how your models are performing in real time. Monitoring is critical for:

- **Proactive Issue Detection**: Identifying latency spikes, high error rates, or resource bottlenecks before they impact the user experience.
- **Continual Optimization**: Using metrics to guide iterative improvements and infrastructure adjustments.
- **Model Drift Detection**: Recognizing when data distribution has changed (concept drift), leading to degraded accuracy or unexpected predictions.

6.2.1 Metrics to Track

1. **Latency**

   - **Definition**: The time from receiving an inference request to returning a prediction.
   - **Significance**: High latency can degrade user experience, especially in real-time or interactive applications.
   - **Measurement**: Track percentile-based metrics (e.g., P50, P90, P99) to capture typical and worst-case scenarios.

2. **Throughput**

   - **Definition**: The number of requests handled per second (RPS).
   - **Significance**: Indicates how many concurrent users or requests your service can handle without degradation.
   - **Measurement**: Often reported as requests or inferences per second; can also measure total CPU/GPU utilization.

3. **Error Rates**

   - **Definition**: The proportion of requests that result in errors (HTTP 4xx/5xx, timeouts, or model-specific exceptions).
   - **Significance**: A rising error rate may indicate bugs, resource exhaustion, or misconfigurations.
   - **Measurement**: Track error types (e.g., 500 Internal Server Error vs. 503 Service Unavailable) to pinpoint causes.

4. **Resource Utilization**

   - **CPU/GPU Usage**: Monitor how fully the processor is being used.
   - **Memory Footprint**: Ensure you aren't running out of RAM/GPU memory.
   - **Disk/Network I/O**: Large or frequent data loads can become bottlenecks.

5. **Model-Specific Quality Metrics**

- **Accuracy, F1-Score, or Other KPIs**: In some cases, you can compare model predictions to ground truth in near real time or periodically.
- **Drift Metrics**: Track input feature distributions or output distributions over time to detect shifts that might degrade model performance.

6.2.2 Tools for Monitoring

1. **Prometheus and Grafana**

   - **Prometheus** is an open-source monitoring system that scrapes metrics from instrumented targets. It's particularly well-suited for containerized microservices.
   - **Grafana** provides a real-time dashboarding solution. You can visualize latency percentiles, throughput, and resource usage in customizable charts.
   - **Integration**: Many ML frameworks and serving solutions can expose Prometheus endpoints with model-level metrics (e.g., TensorFlow Serving).

2. **Application Performance Monitoring (APM)**

   - Commercial tools like **Datadog**, **New Relic**, or **Dynatrace** offer advanced features: distributed tracing, anomaly detection, and alerting.
   - APMs are especially valuable for large enterprise setups with multiple microservices.

3. **Cloud Provider Tooling**

   - **AWS CloudWatch, Google Cloud Monitoring, Azure Monitor**: Each major cloud platform provides native monitoring and logging capabilities.

- These often integrate tightly with autoscaling features, allowing you to scale based on custom metrics.

4. **Custom Dashboards and Alerts**

- For more specialized or domain-specific metrics (e.g., recommendation relevance, chat response quality), teams may build custom dashboards or use open-source solutions like **Kibana** (for log analytics).

6.2.3 Setting Up a Monitoring Pipeline

1. **Metric Collection**

- Instrument your code to expose metrics in a standard format (e.g., Prometheus exposition format).
- Log relevant data (request timestamps, response times, memory usage) to a centralized store.

2. **Visualization**

- Configure dashboards in Grafana, CloudWatch, or your preferred monitoring platform to display real-time charts of key metrics.
- Use historical views to compare current performance against past baselines.

3. **Alerting**

- Define thresholds or anomaly detection rules for critical metrics (e.g., latency > 500ms for 95th percentile, CPU usage > 80%).
- Set up notifications via email, SMS, or Slack so your team can rapidly respond to issues.

4. **Root Cause Analysis**

- When anomalies occur, use tracing tools (like **Jaeger** or **Zipkin** for distributed systems) or logs (e.g., **ELK stack**: Elasticsearch, Logstash,

Kibana) to pinpoint specific bottlenecks or errors.

- Correlate spikes in inference latency with code deployments, model updates, or infrastructure changes to find the cause.

6.3 Putting It All Together

Let's walk through a hypothetical scenario to see how scaling and monitoring come together in practice.

6.3.1 Example Scenario: E-Commerce Recommendation System

Problem: An e-commerce platform uses a product recommendation model. During holiday sales, traffic can spike 10x, causing latency to rise and some requests to fail.

1. **Baseline**

   - The model is optimized via quantization and pruning (from earlier chapters). It runs on four GPU instances in a Kubernetes cluster.

2. **Scaling Strategy**

   - **Autoscaling Policy**: If average GPU utilization exceeds 70% for more than 5 minutes, spin up an additional instance. If it stays below 40% for 10 minutes, scale down one instance.
   - **Caching**: The service caches recommendations for top-selling products to reduce load on the model.

3. **Monitoring Setup**

   - **Prometheus** scrapes metrics from each model-serving pod.
   - **Grafana** dashboard displays real-time latency percentiles (P50, P90, P99), GPU usage, and error rates.

- **Alerting** triggers a Slack message if P99 latency exceeds 300ms for more than 1 minute.

4. **Traffic Spike**

   - As holiday traffic ramps up, GPU usage jumps to 75%. The autoscaler adds 2 more GPU pods.
   - Latency remains within acceptable bounds (under 200ms P90).

5. **Model Drift?**

   - Prometheus tracks the distribution of user features (location, purchase history). Alerts trigger if distributions change drastically— indicating potential model drift.
   - The team notices new product categories gaining popularity; they plan a partial model retraining after the holiday season to update recommendations.

Through effective **scaling** and **monitoring**, the platform maintains consistent performance despite surging demand. The team can quickly identify any performance degradation or data drift, ensuring the recommendation system remains both **fast** and **relevant**.

6.4 Conclusion

Scaling and monitoring are integral components of a **robust** machine learning deployment strategy. Even the most optimized model will struggle under unpredictable real-world conditions if you don't have a plan for handling traffic surges and a system for continuously measuring and improving performance.

- **Scaling** your model-serving infrastructure can be approached horizontally, vertically, or with a combination of both. Tools like Kubernetes, serverless frameworks, and autoscaling policies help you match resources to demand.

- **Monitoring** goes hand-in-hand with scaling. By tracking latency, throughput, error rates, and model-specific metrics, you can detect problems early, maintain a strong user experience, and manage costs effectively.

Next Steps: In **Chapter 7**, we'll review **real-world case studies** of model optimizations—bringing together everything we've covered so far. You'll see how organizations in different industries tackled unique performance challenges, scaled their infrastructure, and continuously monitored success metrics to deliver reliable and cost-effective AI services.

Key Takeaways

1. **Scaling Is a Must**: You can't rely on a single optimized instance to handle all future load; be prepared to grow horizontally (more instances) and vertically (larger nodes).
2. **Autoscaling**: Automate resource provisioning based on metrics (e.g., CPU usage, latency, or domain-specific KPIs) to adapt quickly to traffic changes.
3. **Monitoring**: Effective monitoring is crucial for proactive issue detection and ongoing performance management.
4. **Essential Metrics**: Latency, throughput, error rates, resource utilization, and model-specific quality metrics (accuracy, drift indicators) form the foundation of good observability.
5. **Alerts and Dashboards**: Tools like Prometheus, Grafana, Datadog, or AWS CloudWatch help you visualize and manage large-scale deployments.
6. **Iterative Process**: Continuous monitoring informs re-optimization, retraining, and infrastructure scaling decisions.

By mastering scaling and monitoring, you ensure that your meticulously **optimized models** continue to deliver top-tier performance and reliability in **dynamic** real-world environments.

Chapter 7: Real-World Case Studies

Throughout this book, we've examined a variety of techniques to optimize machine learning models for production deployment, from quantization and pruning to caching, knowledge distillation, and hardware-specific tuning. In this chapter, we'll focus on **practical, real-world examples** of how these optimization strategies come together to solve specific problems.

Each of the following case studies draws from common industry scenarios:

1. **Optimizing a Vision Model for Real-Time Inference**
2. **Reducing Costs for a Chatbot Model**
3. **Scaling an E-Commerce Recommendation System**

In these examples, you'll see how different combinations of techniques—alongside careful measurement, monitoring, and iteration—can yield significant gains in performance, scalability, and cost savings.

7.1 Case Study 1: Optimizing a Vision Model for Real-Time Inference

7.1.1 Problem: High Latency in an Object Detection Application

A startup developed an **object detection** application for surveillance cameras. The model—a large YOLOv5 variant—was deployed on AWS EC2 instances with GPU acceleration. Despite using a GPU, the **inference time per frame** was too high to achieve real-time detection.

- **Symptoms:**

- Latency ranged between 150–200 ms per frame (roughly 5–7 frames per second).
- During peak traffic (multiple video streams), the latency would spike further.
- GPU utilization was high, and the cost of scaling horizontally with more GPU instances was prohibitive.

- **Goal**:

  - **Reduce latency** to under 30 ms per frame (i.e., achieve ~30+ FPS).
  - Keep accuracy at a level sufficient for reliable detection of people, vehicles, and common objects.

7.1.2 Diagnosis

1. **Profiling**:

   - The team used **NVIDIA Nsight Systems** to profile the inference pipeline.
   - Key findings:
     - The model's size and complexity (tens of millions of parameters) caused significant GPU compute overhead.
     - Not all operations were optimized or fused—multiple small kernels led to overhead in kernel launches.

2. **Data Preprocessing**:

   - The input pipeline involved resizing and normalizing frames on the CPU, then transferring them to the GPU. This introduced additional overhead.

7.1.3 Solution: Using TensorRT and Quantization to Achieve a 5x Speedup

1. **Quantization**:

- The team experimented with **FP16** and **INT8** precision using PyTorch's quantization features and TensorRT's calibration.
- **FP16** inference provided a significant speedup with minimal impact on detection accuracy.
- **INT8** required careful calibration but yielded even lower latency. However, the accuracy drop (~2–3 points in mAP) was borderline acceptable.
- Final decision: **FP16** as the primary deployment format, and **INT8** in specific scenarios where a small accuracy loss was tolerable (e.g., non-critical environments).

2. **TensorRT Engine**:

- The model was exported to ONNX, then converted into a TensorRT engine with layer fusion and **kernel auto-tuning**.
- Batch size was set to 1 for real-time single-frame inference, but TensorRT's engine creation still optimized kernel launches for this scenario.
- In some environments, they used a slightly larger batch size (4 or 8) if multiple camera streams could be processed in mini-batches, further improving throughput.

3. **Caching and Pipeline Optimization**:

- **On-GPU Preprocessing**: Instead of resizing frames on the CPU, they leveraged **CUDA** for image scaling and normalization.
- **Asynchronous Data Transfers**: Using CUDA streams allowed overlapping data transfers and GPU computation.

4. **Results**:

- **Latency**: Dropped from 150–200 ms down to ~30 ms (FP16) and ~20 ms (INT8) per frame— a **5–7x speedup**.

- **Accuracy**: mAP reduced by only ~1 point in FP16 mode.
- **Cost Savings**: Fewer GPU instances were needed to handle the same load, reducing cloud expenses.

7.1.4 Key Takeaways

- **Hardware-Specific Optimization Matters**: Leveraging TensorRT's specialized GPU optimizations led to a massive speed boost.
- **Quantization**: Can be a powerful tool for boosting performance if you can afford a minor drop in accuracy.
- **Pipeline Efficiency**: Don't overlook preprocessing overhead. Moving tasks onto the GPU and using asynchronous data transfers can significantly reduce overall latency.

7.2 Case Study 2: Reducing Costs for a Chatbot Model

7.2.1 Problem: High Cloud Costs Due to Inefficient Resource Usage

An established enterprise deployed a **customer-service chatbot** powered by a large language model (LLM) akin to GPT-2. The model ran on multiple GPU instances to handle traffic from the company's website and support portals. Although the chatbot performed well, it was **costing tens of thousands of dollars per month** in GPU usage.

- **Symptoms**:
    - Each instance of the LLM consumed a sizable GPU memory footprint.
    - During off-peak hours, GPU instances remained mostly idle but still incurred high costs.

- Switching to CPU-only instances caused unacceptable latency (over 2 seconds per response).
- **Goal**:

  - Reduce infrastructure costs by at least 50%, without significantly impacting user experience.
  - Maintain latencies within 500 ms for typical user queries.

7.2.2 Diagnosis

1. **Model Analysis**:
   - The LLM had hundreds of millions of parameters. Inference memory usage was high because of large embedding layers and multi-headed attention.
2. **Usage Patterns**:
   - Traffic spiked during business hours, then dropped sharply overnight.
   - The model was underutilized (low GPU utilization) a large portion of the time.

7.2.3 Solution: Pruning and Distillation to Reduce Model Size by 50%

1. **Pruning**:

   - The engineering team used **structured pruning** to remove entire attention heads that contributed little to performance.
   - This required a brief finetuning phase after pruning to recover lost accuracy.
   - **Result**: Model size was reduced by 20–25%, leading to lower GPU memory usage and a slight speedup in inference.
2. **Knowledge Distillation**:

- They trained a **smaller "student" model** (~60% the size of the original GPT-2) to mimic the outputs of the full model.
- Distillation training used both the original dataset and the teacher model's logits.
- **Result**: The student model retained ~95% of the teacher's accuracy (measured by perplexity and next-word prediction metrics).

3. **Autoscaling and Mixed Precision**:

- Implemented **autoscaling** to reduce GPU instances during off-peak hours.
- Moved to **mixed-precision (FP16)** inference, leveraging GPU Tensor Cores to cut inference time by another ~30%.

4. **Overall Outcomes**:

- **50%+ Reduction in Cloud Costs**: Fewer (and smaller) GPU instances were needed.
- **Latency**: Averaged ~400 ms per response, well below the 500 ms goal.
- **User Experience**: Preliminary A/B tests indicated no major drop in user satisfaction; the distilled chatbot performed comparably to the original.

7.2.4 Key Takeaways

- **Model Size Greatly Affects Costs**: Large models can yield high-quality outputs but often come with a hefty price tag in the cloud.
- **Pruning + Distillation**: This combination is especially effective for language models, trimming size while preserving most of the performance.
- **Autoscaling**: Matching resources to demand further optimized spending, especially for variable traffic patterns.

7.3 Case Study 3: Scaling an E-Commerce Recommendation System

7.3.1 Problem: Latency Spikes During Peak Hours

An e-commerce platform ran a **personalized recommendation system** that generated product suggestions on the fly. The service performed well on typical traffic, but experienced **latency spikes** during big promotions and holiday sales. User drop-off increased when recommendations took more than 2 seconds to load.

- **Symptoms**:
    - Peak-hour traffic caused inference latency to exceed 2 seconds.
    - Horizontal scaling did not fully mitigate the issue—some requests still queued up, causing "burst" latency spikes.
    - The recommendation model was relatively large (a wide-and-deep architecture) and frequently accessed the feature store for user data.
- **Goal**:
    - Keep latency under 500 ms for 95% of requests, even at peak loads.
    - Maintain personalization quality— recommendation accuracy was key to boosting sales.

7.3.2 Diagnosis

1. **Bottleneck Analysis**:
    - The team profiled both the **ML inference** and **feature retrieval** processes.
    - Found that retrieving user embedding vectors from a database was adding ~100 ms to each request.

- The model itself took ~300 ms for a single, unoptimized inference step on CPU instances.

2. **Infrastructure**:

   - Running on CPU-optimized instances to reduce costs, but large bursts exceeded CPU capacity.
   - Occasional usage of GPU instances for batch-based recommendations, but these weren't integrated into real-time serving.

7.3.3 Solution: Implementing Caching and Hardware-Aware Optimizations

1. **Caching Frequently Accessed Data**:

   - Implemented **Redis** to cache user profiles and frequently accessed features.
   - Reduced the average feature retrieval time from ~100 ms to ~5 ms.

2. **Hybrid Serving on CPUs and GPUs**:

   - Adopted a **split** architecture:
     - CPU-based nodes handle typical traffic and "simple" recommendations (returning a set of top picks for casual browsing).
     - GPU-based nodes handle more complex requests during peak or for high-value users requiring deeper personalization.
   - Deployed an autoscaling policy that spun up GPU instances when CPU-based inference queue times exceeded a threshold.

3. **Quantization**:

   - Enabled **int8 quantization** for CPU inference on widely available operators (using ONNX Runtime's quantization tooling).
   - CPU inference time dropped from ~300 ms to ~180 ms per request.

4. **Batching**:

- For GPU-based nodes, requests arriving within a short time window (e.g., 100 ms) were **batched** to run in a single forward pass. This significantly improved throughput during bursts.

5. **Outcomes**:

  - **Latency**: 95th percentile fell below 500 ms. During Black Friday sales, the system scaled to meet 3x normal traffic without exceeding 1 second latency.
  - **Revenue Impact**: The improved responsiveness correlated with a +5% lift in sales conversions.
  - **Resource Efficiency**: Running mixed CPU/GPU infrastructure and caching effectively balanced cost and performance.

7.3.4 Key Takeaways

- **Data Access Bottlenecks**: Don't overlook feature retrieval times; caching or feature store optimizations can dramatically lower overhead.
- **Hybrid Deployments**: Using both CPU and GPU instances can align cost with demand, reserving the more expensive resources for peak loads or complex tasks.
- **Batching**: Short bursts of traffic can be aggregated into mini-batches on GPUs, improving throughput significantly without sacrificing too much latency.

7.4 Conclusion

These case studies demonstrate how **real-world constraints** —latency requirements, cost pressures, unpredictable user traffic—shape the model optimization and deployment strategies that teams adopt. By combining the techniques covered in earlier chapters:

1. **Quantization** and **Pruning** can reduce compute load and memory usage.
2. **Knowledge Distillation** maintains performance with a smaller footprint.
3. **Caching** and **Preprocessing** optimizations reduce end-to-end latency.
4. **Hardware-Aware** deployment ensures you leverage the strengths of CPUs, GPUs, or TPUs effectively.
5. **Autoscaling** and **Monitoring** let you handle peak demands and maintain consistent performance over time.

The common thread in these examples is **iterative optimization** guided by continuous measurement:

- Identify bottlenecks using profiling tools.
- Experiment with different techniques (e.g., quantization, knowledge distillation) to find the right balance between speed, size, and accuracy.
- Validate gains through A/B testing or real user metrics.
- Monitor and adjust resource allocation dynamically in response to changing traffic patterns or new user behaviors.

Key Takeaways

1. **No "One Size Fits All"**: Each application has unique constraints—choose the optimization and scaling strategies best suited for your scenario.
2. **Measure, Optimize, Measure Again**: Profiling and monitoring are essential to identify bottlenecks and validate improvements.
3. **Combine Techniques**: The biggest gains often come from **layering** multiple optimizations (e.g., pruning + distillation + caching).
4. **Keep an Eye on Accuracy**: Always track potential trade-offs in model performance. Some losses in accuracy may be acceptable; others can be critical.

5. **Cost vs. Performance**: ROI-driven decisions matter. Optimize where it counts—especially if cloud expenses are a significant part of your budget.

Moving forward, we'll explore **future trends in model optimization** (Chapter 8), covering emerging hardware accelerators, AutoML systems, and the growing role of edge computing. These real-world stories provide a solid foundation for appreciating how fast the field evolves—and why staying attuned to new techniques and tools is essential for sustained success.

Chapter 8: Future Trends in Model Optimization

The field of machine learning continues to advance at a rapid pace, and with it comes a growing need for innovative ways to optimize models for deployment. As applications become more sophisticated, data volumes grow, and latency requirements tighten, the traditional methods we've explored thus far will evolve—and entirely new optimization avenues will emerge. In this chapter, we look ahead to **future trends** that are likely to shape model optimization in the coming years:

1. **The Rise of AI Hardware Accelerators** – Dedicated chips and specialized architectures designed for machine learning workloads.
2. **AutoML and Automated Optimization Pipelines** – New tools and platforms that automate much of the tuning and optimization process.
3. **The Role of Edge Computing in Optimization** – Dealing with latency and connectivity constraints by pushing inference closer to end users and devices.

We'll see how each of these trends reflects a broader push toward **efficiency, scalability, and flexibility** in AI deployments, ultimately offering new ways to balance performance, cost, and accuracy.

8.1 The Rise of AI Hardware Accelerators

Traditional CPUs and GPUs have been the backbone of AI deployments for many years, but as model sizes balloon and real-time performance demands intensify, **specialized hardware accelerators** are quickly becoming mainstream. These accelerators tackle some of the inherent inefficiencies in general-purpose hardware, delivering **higher throughput**, **lower power consumption**, and **reduced latency** for specific machine learning tasks.

8.1.1 Types of AI Accelerators

1. **ASICs (Application-Specific Integrated Circuits)**

   - **Definition**: Custom silicon chips designed for a particular application or algorithm (e.g., Google's Tensor Processing Unit, or TPU).
   - **Advantages**:
     - Highly optimized for certain operations (matrix multiplications, convolutions).
     - Can offer large performance gains and energy efficiency compared to GPUs.
   - **Limitations**:
     - Less flexibility; changing models or algorithms can require new hardware iterations.
     - Typically require specialized ecosystems or frameworks.

2. **FPGAs (Field-Programmable Gate Arrays)**

   - **Definition**: Reconfigurable chips that can be programmed (in hardware description languages) to accelerate specific workloads.
   - **Advantages**:
     - Flexible; can be updated to support evolving model architectures.
     - Potentially lower power usage than GPUs for some tasks.
   - **Limitations**:
     - Steep learning curve to program and optimize.
     - Not as plug-and-play as GPU-based solutions.

3. **Next-Gen GPU Architectures**

   - **Definition**: GPUs continue to evolve, incorporating specialized tensor cores

(NVIDIA), matrix cores (AMD), or other dedicated AI acceleration blocks.

- **Advantages**:
    - Broad software support and familiarity.
    - Strong ecosystems (CUDA, ROCm, etc.).
- **Limitations**:
    - Still general-purpose in many respects, so not as power-efficient as custom ASICs for targeted tasks.

4. **Neuromorphic Chips**

- **Definition**: A more experimental class of hardware that mimics the structure of biological neural networks.
- **Advantages**:
    - Very promising for low-power, event-driven tasks (like sensor processing).
    - Could potentially enable always-on AI at the edge.
- **Limitations**:
    - Still in research phases; limited commercial adoption and tooling.

8.1.2 Impact on Model Optimization

As these accelerators gain traction, **model optimization** will increasingly include a stage of **hardware selection** or **hardware-specific compilation**. We can expect:

- **Framework Integration**: Toolchains like Apache TVM, XLA, and vendor-provided compilers will keep evolving to target these specialized chips, allowing developers to automatically optimize their models for each hardware platform.
- **Finer-Grained Precision**: Some accelerators will support data types beyond FP16 or INT8, like BF16, FP8, or custom integer formats. This drives **hardware-aware quantization** as a first-class optimization strategy.

- **Shifts in Model Architecture**: Certain architectures will be favored for their compatibility with accelerator hardware (e.g., more matrix-heavy layers or more "friendly" layer types that can be easily parallelized).

The result is a **dynamic feedback loop**: new hardware designs inspire new model optimizations, and emerging models push the boundaries of hardware innovation.

8.2 AutoML and Automated Optimization Pipelines

AutoML (Automated Machine Learning) originally focused on automating hyperparameter tuning and model selection. However, modern AutoML systems are expanding into **end-to-end pipelines** that include data preprocessing, feature engineering, neural architecture search (NAS), and—crucially—**model optimization for deployment**.

8.2.1 Automated Neural Architecture Search

1. **NAS Basics**

   - Instead of manually designing architectures, NAS algorithms search a large space of possible network configurations (e.g., different layer types, widths, or connections).
   - The goal is to find models that strike the best balance between **accuracy** and **efficiency** (latency, memory footprint).

2. **Hardware-In-The-Loop Optimization**

   - Some NAS frameworks directly measure hardware performance (inference time or power consumption) for candidate architectures.
   - The search algorithm rewards architectures that meet latency or energy constraints, effectively **co-designing** the model and hardware usage.

3. **Tools and Frameworks**

- **Google AutoML, Microsoft NNI, Ray Tune, AutoGluon,** and **KubeFlow** are popular platforms that integrate varying degrees of NAS and hyperparameter search.
- Many support custom metrics—like throughput or model size—to guide the search toward practical deployment goals.

8.2.2 Pipeline-Oriented Optimization

1. **Data-Driven Optimization**

- Automated pipelines handle tasks like feature selection, data augmentation, and dimensionality reduction that can lead to smaller, simpler models from the start.
- For example, an AutoML system might detect high-correlation features and drop redundant features, enabling a more compact network downstream.

2. **Automated Quantization and Pruning**

- Some frameworks (e.g., **TensorFlow Model Optimization Toolkit, PyTorch FX**-based tools) integrate pruning or quantization passes into the training loop automatically.
- Instead of manually deciding pruning thresholds or quantization strategies, the system experiments with different configurations and picks the best one.

3. **One-Click Deployment**

- These pipelines often end with a "deploy" step that packages your model with optimized runtime configurations (e.g., TensorRT engines or TFLite binaries) for immediate production use.

- This reduces the engineering overhead of translating a proof-of-concept model into a fully optimized, production-ready artifact.

8.2.3 The Upside and Challenges of AutoML

- **Upside**:
  - **Time Savings**: Data scientists can focus on problem framing and data quality, leaving the grunt work of model tuning to an automated system.
  - **Systematic Search**: AutoML can sometimes discover surprising architectures or optimization settings that human intuition might overlook.
- **Challenges**:
  - **Compute Costs**: NAS and other AutoML strategies can be extremely resource-intensive.
  - **Overfitting to Benchmarks**: AutoML might overfit to a specific validation set or hardware configuration if not carefully generalized.
  - **Black-Box Solutions**: AutoML can produce architectures that are hard to interpret or maintain if the system doesn't provide transparency.

AutoML is poised to become even more capable, potentially making **human-in-the-loop** model optimization less necessary—though expert oversight will likely remain important for high-stakes applications.

8.3 The Role of Edge Computing in Optimization

As sensor-rich devices (e.g., IoT sensors, smartphones, AR/VR headsets) proliferate, the need for **edge computing** solutions grows. Instead of sending all data to a cloud data center for processing, **edge-based models** can perform inference locally, reducing latency and bandwidth usage. This shift has profound implications for how we optimize models.

8.3.1 Why Edge Computing?

1. **Latency Sensitivity**

   - Applications such as autonomous vehicles, robotics, and real-time analytics require response times of milliseconds, making round-trip to the cloud unfeasible.

2. **Privacy and Bandwidth**

   - Keeping data local can alleviate privacy concerns and reduce network costs, especially when dealing with video or sensor streams.

3. **Offline Capabilities**

   - Edge devices can continue functioning even with poor or no connectivity.

8.3.2 Challenges for Edge Optimization

1. **Limited Compute and Memory**

   - Edge devices often have far less RAM and processing power than data-center servers (though specialized edge accelerators are emerging).
   - Models must be **highly compressed**—through pruning, quantization, or distillation—to fit within hardware constraints.

2. **Power Constraints**

   - Battery-operated devices (smartphones, wearable sensors) require **energy-efficient inference**. Techniques like **dynamic batching** or **spiking neural networks** (in neuromorphic hardware) might become more common.

3. **Diverse Hardware Ecosystems**

- The edge landscape is fragmented, with different ARM CPU variants, mobile GPUs, DSPs, and NPUs. This fragmentation complicates one-size-fits-all optimization solutions.

8.3.3 Edge-First Model Design

1. **TinyML**

   - A subfield focusing on deploying deep learning models on microcontrollers and ultra-low-power devices.
   - Tools like **TensorFlow Lite Micro** or **Edge Impulse** provide specialized workflows to fit neural networks into kilobytes of memory.

2. **On-Device Training**

   - As devices become more powerful, some workloads will include **federated learning** or **on-device fine-tuning**, necessitating further optimizations to handle incremental updates efficiently.

3. **Progressive Inference**

   - Splitting a model into stages: a small first-stage model runs on-device, quickly filtering out simple cases. If more complex processing is needed, data is sent to a cloud-based, heavier model.
   - This approach reduces average inference cost and latency for common, less complex tasks.

8.4 Putting It All Together: The Future of Optimized AI

As **AI accelerators** mature, **AutoML** pipelines become more sophisticated, and **edge computing** grows in importance, we'll see a confluence of trends:

1. **Hardware-Software Co-Design**

    - Model developers will collaborate with hardware teams (or use advanced compilers) to shape architectures that map well to specific accelerators.
    - We can anticipate more synergy between model architectures (e.g., sparse networks, attention mechanisms) and hardware features (e.g., specialized matrix engines, on-chip memory).

2. **Highly Distributed Systems**

    - AI deployments will increasingly span **edge devices, on-premises servers, and cloud clusters**. Data may be partially processed at the edge and then aggregated in the cloud.
    - Optimizations will need to consider **end-to-end** pipelines, ensuring synergy between the edge-based steps and the cloud-based ones.

3. **Automation and Continuous Optimization**

    - Automated pipelines will reduce the need for manual tuning, but continuous monitoring (as covered in Chapter 6) remains crucial to detect drift and changing usage patterns.
    - ML teams will spend more time on domain-specific considerations—like defining custom optimization metrics for their specific industry or use case—and less time on routine engineering tasks.

4. **Sustainability and Green AI**

    - Large-scale AI consumes substantial energy. Expect an increasing focus on **sustainable AI**, where model optimization and hardware selection also account for carbon footprints.
    - Techniques like pruning, quantization, and distillation may be reframed as ways to reduce environmental impact alongside cost.

8.5 Conclusion

The future of model optimization will be shaped by **accelerator hardware**, **automated pipelines**, and **edge-centric architectures**. Each represents a strategic opportunity for practitioners:

- **Leverage Specialized Hardware**: Whether using TPUs, custom ASICs, or the latest GPUs, matching your workloads to the right accelerator can yield dramatic improvements.
- **Automate Wherever Possible**: AutoML and advanced compilers reduce manual effort and can discover optimizations that humans miss.
- **Push Intelligence to the Edge**: As more devices operate in real-world environments, edge deployments will demand models that are extremely efficient yet reliable.

These trends emphasize a **holistic** approach to AI: from model design and data pipelines to hardware selection and continuous monitoring, all aspects must work in tandem to deliver fast, cost-effective, and sustainable machine learning solutions.

Key Takeaways

1. **Specialized Hardware**: From ASICs to FPGAs and next-gen GPUs, AI accelerators will continue to diversify, driving new optimization techniques.
2. **AutoML Evolution**: Automated neural architecture search, quantization, and pruning pipelines will make optimization more accessible—at the cost of higher compute overhead during the search process.
3. **Edge Focus**: As latency, bandwidth, and privacy concerns grow, edge computing will demand ultra-compact, low-power models. This spurs growth in TinyML and federated learning.

4. **Continuous Innovation**: The arms race between model complexity and optimization techniques will persist. Stay informed about new hardware features, compilers, and frameworks.
5. **Sustainability**: Optimization isn't just about speed and cost anymore; reducing energy consumption and carbon footprint is becoming a core priority.

With an eye on these emerging trends, you'll be well-positioned to build and maintain machine learning systems that thrive in a fast-changing technological landscape—balancing performance, resource efficiency, and adaptability for whatever challenges the future holds.

Conclusion

Optimizing machine learning models for deployment is a critical undertaking that bridges the gap between research prototypes and production-ready solutions. In this book, we embarked on a comprehensive exploration of the techniques, tools, and best practices that enable high-performance, reliable, and cost-effective AI services in real-world environments.

We began by emphasizing the **importance of model optimization** and delved into the **model deployment lifecycle**, identifying where and when optimization can yield the greatest returns. We then surveyed a range of **optimization techniques**—quantization, pruning, knowledge distillation, and caching—each offering unique trade-offs between speed, memory footprint, and accuracy. Building on this foundation, we examined **tools and frameworks** (TensorRT, ONNX Runtime, TensorFlow Lite, and Apache TVM) that streamline the optimization process, allowing you to adapt models to diverse hardware backends with relative ease.

We also explored **hardware-specific optimizations**, showing how CPUs, GPUs, and TPUs demand different strategies to achieve peak performance, and highlighted the role of **profiling** to detect bottlenecks. **Scaling and monitoring** took center stage next, as no amount of model optimization alone can handle unpredictable growth in demand or ensure ongoing reliability; autoscaling strategies and continuous monitoring are indispensable for robust, user-facing AI services. Finally, we examined **real-world case studies** to see how teams across various industries combine these techniques to deliver responsive, cost-effective, and high-accuracy solutions—and looked at **future trends** such as specialized AI accelerators, automated optimization pipelines, and the expanding role of edge computing.

Below are key insights that unify these chapters into a cohesive framework for continual success in model deployment:

---

1. Optimization Is Iterative, Not One-Time

Regardless of your application—be it computer vision, NLP, or recommendation systems—optimization is an ongoing process. New data, hardware upgrades, and shifting user demands require you to **revisit** your optimization pipeline. Techniques like pruning or distillation can be re-applied each time you retrain or finetune, ensuring your models remain both fast and accurate.

2. Measurement and Profiling Drive Improvements

The mantra of **"measure, optimize, measure again"** applies throughout the entire lifecycle. Profiling tools—whether NVIDIA Nsight for GPUs or built-in profilers for CPU-bound workloads—help you pinpoint bottlenecks and validate that each optimization actually delivers performance gains. Without data-driven insights, you risk investing effort in changes that don't produce tangible results.

3. Hardware and Framework Choices Matter

Modern AI deployments span CPUs, GPUs, TPUs, edge accelerators, and more. Each hardware type demands nuanced optimizations, from leveraging vectorized libraries on CPUs to mixed-precision on GPUs and quantized inference on specialized ASICs. Meanwhile, frameworks like TensorRT, ONNX Runtime, TensorFlow Lite, and Apache TVM automate much of the heavy lifting—**but** success depends on selecting the right tools for your target environment.

4. Scale and Monitoring Are Essential for Production

Even the best-optimized model can falter under unexpected traffic surges or data shifts. **Autoscaling** ensures your infrastructure can expand and contract to match demand, while **monitoring** (via Prometheus, Grafana, or cloud-native APMs) guards against performance degradation, errors, and model drift. This synergy of scaling and visibility keeps your system robust in real-world conditions.

5. Real-World Results Require Multilayered Solutions

The case studies highlighted that **no single technique** is a silver bullet—companies often blend quantization, pruning, caching, and hardware-aware strategies to achieve the right balance of cost and latency. Sometimes, advanced solutions like knowledge distillation or specialized GPU/TPU optimizations are critical to meeting strict service-level agreements (SLAs).

6. The Future Will Be Even More Flexible, Automated, and Edge-Centric

Looking ahead, we see trends like **AI accelerators** that push performance boundaries, **AutoML** that automates model and hardware co-design, and **edge computing** that brings inference closer to the data source. These innovations will further shape how we think about optimization. They also underscore a broader push to **integrate AI into every aspect of modern technology**—from tiny wearable devices to massive data centers.

Final Thoughts

Whether you're a data scientist, ML engineer, or technical leader, the insights and methods outlined in these chapters empower you to build **highly efficient machine learning**

pipelines that thrive under real-world constraints. Key takeaways include:

- **Adopt a lifecycle perspective**: Optimization isn't just a post-training afterthought; it intersects with each stage of development and deployment.
- **Be systematic**: Use profiling and benchmarking to guide decisions, ensuring each step is grounded in data.
- **Leverage specialized tools**: Frameworks and compilers can drastically reduce manual effort while unlocking hardware-accelerated performance.
- **Plan for growth and variability**: Have autoscaling and monitoring in place to handle evolving demands and detect issues quickly.
- **Stay adaptive**: Remain alert to new hardware innovations and evolving best practices—tomorrow's breakthroughs will further reshape how we optimize.

By synthesizing the technical approaches presented here with a culture of continuous experimentation and learning, you'll be well-prepared to deliver machine learning models that **excel** in deployment—meeting user expectations for speed, reliability, and cost-effectiveness in the face of ever-increasing scale and complexity.

Appendix

Below is a detailed **Appendix** designed to supplement the main content of this book. It consolidates key terminology, introduces an extensive list of tools and libraries referenced throughout, and provides further reading and resources to support continued learning and experimentation in model optimization.

Appendix A: Glossary of Optimization Terms

Accuracy

A measure of how often a model's predictions are correct. The specific definition depends on the problem type (e.g., for classification tasks, accuracy is the fraction of correct predictions over total predictions).

AutoML

Short for "Automated Machine Learning." Refers to systems that automate various stages of the machine learning workflow, from feature engineering to neural architecture search, often including optimization steps.

Batch Size

The number of samples processed simultaneously in one forward/backward pass during training or inference. Larger batch sizes can improve parallel efficiency but may also increase memory usage and can affect latency in real-time inference scenarios.

BF16 (bfloat16)

A 16-bit floating-point format with the same exponent range as 32-bit floats (FP32) but fewer bits for the significand.

Balances performance gains similar to FP16 with a reduced risk of numerical underflow/overflow.

Cache Invalidation

The process of updating or removing data in a cache that has become stale or outdated, ensuring that clients receive correct and up-to-date information from a caching layer.

Concept Drift

A shift in the statistical properties of the target variable or features over time, leading to a mismatch between the training data and real-world data. Models experiencing concept drift may degrade in accuracy unless they are retrained or updated.

Distillation Loss

A metric (often KL divergence) used to measure how closely a student model's output distribution matches that of a larger teacher model in knowledge distillation.

Distributed Tracing

A monitoring technique that tracks requests across multiple microservices or components, providing end-to-end visibility into latencies and bottlenecks. Tools like Jaeger or Zipkin are commonly used for distributed tracing.

Dynamic Quantization

A quantization technique where model weights are stored in a lower-precision format (e.g., INT8), but activations are quantized "on the fly" during inference based on observed ranges of the input data.

Edge Computing

A paradigm where data processing and model inference happen on edge devices (e.g., smartphones, embedded systems) rather than in centralized cloud servers. Reduces latency and bandwidth usage but requires highly optimized, compact models.

Federated Learning

A form of distributed machine learning where models are trained across multiple decentralized devices or servers, each holding local data samples, without sharing raw data among parties.

FP16 (Half-Precision)

A 16-bit floating-point format used to reduce the memory footprint and boost compute throughput. Widely used on GPUs that support half-precision arithmetic through specialized tensor cores.

Graph Optimization

Any technique that modifies or fuses the computational graph of a model (e.g., removing redundant nodes, combining operations) for faster execution and reduced memory overhead.

Hardware-In-The-Loop (HIL) Optimization

An approach in Neural Architecture Search or model optimization that measures real-world hardware performance (e.g., latency, power consumption) and uses these measurements to guide the optimization process.

Knowledge Distillation

A technique in which a smaller student model is trained to replicate the behavior of a larger teacher model. Often used to reduce model size and improve inference speed while retaining most of the teacher model's accuracy.

Latency

The time it takes to process one request from input to output. For real-time applications (e.g., online recommendation, video processing), low latency is often critical.

Load Balancer

A network device or software layer that distributes incoming requests across multiple servers or model instances to prevent any single node from becoming a bottleneck.

Mixed Precision

A training or inference approach that uses multiple numerical precisions (e.g., FP16 for certain layers, FP32 for others) to balance speed and numerical stability.

Model Drift

See **Concept Drift**. Sometimes "model drift" is used interchangeably, though concept drift usually refers more specifically to shifts in the underlying data distributions.

ONNX (Open Neural Network Exchange)

An open standard format for representing machine learning models that allows interoperability between different frameworks (e.g., PyTorch, TensorFlow) and inference engines (e.g., ONNX Runtime, TensorRT).

Pipeline

A series of steps (data loading, preprocessing, model inference, post-processing) that an input must pass through to produce an output. Optimizing the pipeline holistically can often yield significant latency reductions.

Pruning

The removal of parameters (weights or filters) in a neural network that contribute little to final predictions. Pruning reduces model size, can improve speed on certain hardware, and sometimes acts as a form of regularization.

Quantization

Converting floating-point parameters (and sometimes activations) into lower-precision representations (e.g., INT8).

Primarily used to reduce model size and accelerate inference, often with a small accuracy trade-off.

Resource Utilization

A measure of how fully your system's resources (CPU, GPU, memory, disk I/O, network) are being used. High utilization may indicate efficiency—or a potential bottleneck if it impedes scalability.

Sparsity

A property of having many zero-valued parameters in a model. Structured or unstructured pruning can exploit sparsity to reduce computation and memory requirements.

Throughput

The number of inferences or requests that a system can handle per unit time (e.g., images per second, requests per second). Throughput metrics often help size infrastructure for peak loads.

TPU (Tensor Processing Unit)

A custom ASIC developed by Google for accelerating machine learning workloads, especially large-scale TensorFlow models. Offers high throughput for matrix operations, used extensively in research and large-scale production.

Unstructured vs. Structured Pruning

- **Unstructured Pruning**: Removes individual weights that have low magnitude. Can lead to very sparse matrices.
- **Structured Pruning**: Removes entire filters, channels, or neurons, making the resulting network more hardware-friendly for acceleration.

Appendix B: List of Tools and Libraries

This appendix provides a consolidated reference of the tools and libraries mentioned throughout the book, organized by category for quick access.

B.1 Frameworks and General Libraries

1. **TensorFlow**

   - A comprehensive machine learning framework known for its computational graph optimization, large ecosystem, and tight integration with Keras for high-level model development.

2. **PyTorch**

   - A popular deep learning framework featuring dynamic computation graphs, an intuitive Pythonic interface, and strong community support.

3. **scikit-learn**

   - A mature Python library for classical machine learning algorithms (regression, classification, clustering) with a user-friendly API.

4. **Apache Spark**

   - A distributed computing framework that can handle large-scale data processing and includes libraries for ML pipelines (Spark MLlib).

B.2 Model Optimization Toolkits

1. **TensorFlow Model Optimization Toolkit**

   - Includes APIs for pruning, quantization, and clustering of TensorFlow models, as well as TensorFlow Lite conversions.

2. **PyTorch Quantization and Pruning**

- Native support in PyTorch for dynamic and static quantization, channel pruning, and experimental structured pruning flows.

3. **OpenVINO**

   - Intel's toolkit for optimizing and deploying models on Intel CPUs, GPUs, and specialized accelerators. It includes post-training quantization and model conversion tools.

4. **NVIDIA TensorRT**

   - High-performance deep learning inference optimizer and runtime for NVIDIA GPUs, with capabilities like layer fusion, mixed-precision, and calibration-based INT8 inference.

5. **ONNX Runtime**

   - A cross-platform inference engine for ONNX models. Offers execution providers for CPUs, GPUs, and other specialized hardware, with built-in optimization passes and quantization tooling.

6. **Apache TVM**

   - A compiler stack that optimizes deep learning models for various CPU, GPU, and specialized accelerator backends. Includes automated tuning frameworks for improved performance.

B.3 Profiling and Monitoring

1. **NVIDIA Nsight Systems / Nsight Compute**

   - Profiling tools for NVIDIA GPUs, providing insights into kernel execution, memory usage, and potential bottlenecks.

2. **PyTorch Profiler / TensorBoard**

   - Built-in profilers that help visualize and analyze the performance of PyTorch or TensorFlow models.

3. **Prometheus**

- An open-source monitoring system and time-series database that scrapes metrics from instrumented endpoints, ideal for containerized microservices.

4. **Grafana**

   - A real-time dashboarding platform that works with Prometheus (and other data sources) to visualize performance metrics and set up alerts.

5. **Datadog / New Relic / Dynatrace**

   - Commercial APM solutions offering advanced distributed tracing, anomaly detection, and performance dashboards.

B.4 Deployment and Containerization

1. **Docker**

   - A widely used containerization platform for packaging applications and dependencies into reproducible, lightweight units.

2. **Kubernetes**

   - An orchestration framework for managing containerized applications at scale, including automated deployment, scaling, and load balancing.

3. **Serverless Platforms**

   - AWS Lambda, Google Cloud Functions, Azure Functions—managed compute services that simplify autoscaling by running code in response to events.

B.5 Edge and Mobile Libraries

1. **TensorFlow Lite**

   - A lighter runtime for TensorFlow models on mobile and embedded devices, with support for quantization and hardware delegates (GPU, NNAPI).

2. **ONNX Runtime Mobile**

   - A version of ONNX Runtime optimized for mobile devices, focusing on reduced binary size and efficient inference on ARM CPUs.

3. **Edge Impulse**

   - A platform for building and deploying TinyML models on microcontrollers, providing an end-to-end pipeline from data acquisition to deployment.

Appendix C: Additional Resources and Reading

The machine learning landscape evolves quickly, and staying updated on new research, tools, and best practices is essential. Below are suggested resources for deepening your understanding of optimization, deployment, and the broader ecosystem.

C.1 Books and Publications

1. **Deep Learning** by Ian Goodfellow, Yoshua Bengio, and Aaron Courville (MIT Press)

   - A foundational text covering deep learning fundamentals, including mathematical underpinnings and advanced techniques.

2. **Hands-On Machine Learning with Scikit-Learn, Keras, and TensorFlow** by Aurélien Géron (O'Reilly)

   - Offers practical guidance on using modern libraries and tools, including some sections on optimization and deployment.

3. **Neural Network Quantization and Pruning** (various research papers)

- Look for works by Song Han, Geoffrey Hinton, and others at top conferences like NeurIPS, ICML, ICLR.

C.2 Online Courses and Tutorials

1. **Fast.ai's Deep Learning Courses**

   - Free, code-centric courses covering cutting-edge techniques in model training and deployment, often leveraging PyTorch.

2. **Coursera's "Deploying Machine Learning Models" Specializations**

   - Several sequences focus on ML engineering best practices, including productionization and optimization.

3. **NVIDIA Deep Learning Institute (DLI)**

   - Hands-on courses that teach CUDA, TensorRT, mixed-precision training, and other GPU-optimized workflows.

C.3 Blogs, Articles, and White Papers

1. **NVIDIA Developer Blog**

   - Features in-depth posts on GPU optimizations, TensorRT releases, and real-world performance benchmarks.

2. **Google AI Blog**

   - Insights into TensorFlow, TPU use cases, and AutoML developments, including best practices for large-scale model deployments.

3. **AWS / Azure / Google Cloud Documentation**

   - Official cloud provider docs often include deployment patterns, reference architectures, and optimization tips for respective infrastructures.

4. **arXiv.org**

- A repository of preprints where researchers publish the latest findings in model compression, NAS, quantization, and more.

C.4 Conferences and Workshops

- **NeurIPS (Neural Information Processing Systems)**
- **ICLR (International Conference on Learning Representations)**
- **ICML (International Conference on Machine Learning)**
- **CVPR (Conference on Computer Vision and Pattern Recognition)**
- **MLSys (Conference on Machine Learning and Systems)**
- **SysML / MLSys Workshops on Efficient ML**

These conferences often host workshops and tutorials focused on the newest techniques in model optimization, hardware acceleration, and deployment.

C.5 Community and Open Source

1. **GitHub**

   - Search for open-source implementations of state-of-the-art compression, quantization, and pruning techniques. Issues and PRs can provide valuable insights into real-world challenges and solutions.

2. **Slack / Discord Communities**

   - TensorFlow, PyTorch, and ONNX each have community channels where professionals share troubleshooting tips and emerging optimizations.

3. **Stack Overflow**

   - A go-to platform for debugging specific issues with frameworks, libraries, or advanced optimization tasks. Look for tags like

```
#pytorch-quantization,
#tensorflow-lite, #onnx-runtime.
```

4. **Kaggle**

- Although known for data science competitions, Kaggle forums sometimes contain advanced discussions on inference speed, memory constraints, and model compression strategies.

How to Use These Appendices

- **Glossary**: Refer back whenever you encounter an unfamiliar optimization term or need clarity on definitions.
- **Tools and Libraries**: Use this list as a starting point to explore frameworks and solutions that fit your specific optimization scenario or hardware environment.
- **Additional Resources**: Extend your knowledge beyond this book with recommended readings, tutorials, and research publications. The field moves quickly, so staying engaged with the broader community will help you keep pace with the latest advancements.

By leveraging these appendices, you can deepen your understanding of key concepts, accelerate your project setup with the right tools, and continue learning from the wealth of resources available in the machine learning ecosystem.